What Will We Do Without Bob?

Coping With the Loss of a Friend
or Loved One

Danny Goddard

Copyright © 2011

ISBN: 978-1-947671-51-5

Dust Jacket Press
PO Box 721243
Oklahoma City, OK 73172
www.dustjacket.com <http://www.dustjacket.com>
800-495-0192

Cover Design: Rick Guilfoil
Graphic Design: Lyn Rayn

Printed in the United States of America. All rights reserved under International Copyright Law. Contents and/or cover may not be reproduced in whole or in part in any form without th eexpress written consent of the Publisher.

Unless otherwise indicated, all Scripture quotations are from the Holy Bible, New International Version® (NIV®), Copyright © 1973, 1978, 1984 International Bible Society. Used by permission of Zondervan. All rights reserved.

Scripture taken from The Message. The Message (MSG), Copyright © 1993, 1994, 1995, 1996, 2000, 2001, 2002 by Eugene H. Peterson.

In memory of my good friend, Bob Jung.
He made music for all of us to enjoy.

Dedicated to Kathryn and her children,
Beverly, Ron, and Don

Contents

Acknowledgements		7
Foreword by Dr. Harold Ivan Smith		9
Introduction: Troubled		13
1.	We'll Never Be the Same	19
2.	We'll Keep Laughing Through Life	29
3.	We'll Keep Loving Jesus	39
4.	We'll Keep Listening to the Music	47
5.	We'll Keep Counting on the Comforter	57
6.	We'll Keep Shedding Some Tears	65
7.	We'll Keep Facing the Holidays	73
8.	We'll Keep Thanking God	83
9.	We'll Keep Going at Our Own Pace	91
10.	We'll Keep Touching Others	101
11.	Conclusion	109
Notes		113
Author Bio		115

Acknowledgments

I thank my God every time I remember you.
(Philippians 1:3, NIV)

The Message seems to have captured the sentiments of the Apostle Paul with its translation of Philippians 1:3, "Every time you cross my mind, I break out in exclamations of thanks to God." That's the way I feel today. A project such as this is not possible without the help of many people. I would like the privilege of expressing my thanks to a few of them . . .

First and foremost, I thank God Who has called me and the Holy Spirit Who equips me to help others in their time of grief. The ministry of comforting the bereaved is not something I have pursued, yet it is that with which I seem to have been entrusted. I also thank my Lord and Savior, Jesus Christ, Who gave His life for us, yet did not stay dead, giving you and me comfort and hope for difficult days.

I thank my wife, Sandie, and my son and daughter-in-law, Tommy and Micha, for believing in me and encouraging me to complete this project.

My appreciation goes to my friend, Dr. Stan Toler, General Superintendent in the Church of the Nazarene. Over the years, he has believed in me, inspired me, and encouraged me to write. I also thank the good people at Dust Jacket, especially Rick Guilfoil and Adam Toler, for publishing this manuscript and I thank Gwen Rodgers of Southern Nazarene University for her technical support with those "pesky end notes."

What an honor it is to have Harold Ivan Smith write the foreword for this book. We have all read and have grown from his writings. Without a doubt, he is the expert when it comes to grief and bereavement. I express to him my deepest gratitude.

Finally, I thank the family of my friend, the late Bob Jung. He was the inspiration for this project and I appreciate his family's giving me the approval to proceed. May the words on these pages be anointed by the Spirit to help someone in need.

—Danny Goddard
New Castle, IN

Foreword

I had finished four days in Miami with 800 grief counselors from around the world; the theorists had offered new insights and the clinicians had shared new techniques and skills to use with grievers. Although I was tired of talking—*and thinking*—about death, I had promised Pastor Goddard that I would write the foreword for this book. I was not far into reading the manuscript when I realized the timing was perfect.

In listening to statistical analysis of a group of grievers (N = 20 or 100 or 976 or whatever), I overlooked one reality: those making up the *N* in academic studies had names and faces and stories like Bob Jung. I never met Bob Jung but by the end of the book I felt like I had. I can understand why the organ's silence is so profound. As I read I started thinking of the people in my life who have been like Bob Jung. And I thought about their absence. But, as I kept reading, I thought about the gifts my Bob Jungs had given me.

This is an important book because God is always accompanying us through our grief and inviting us to what's next. The great question is not Why? (although that is a permissible question) but "Now what?" The Psalmist's question, "How do we sing the Lord's song in a strange land" (137:4) or in the land of grief is still *the question*. And is the underlying question in Goddard's sensitive writing. While I had read that Psalm fragment many times, I somehow had the belief that their captors had taken away their harps. No! The Israelites hung up their harps "on the willows."

This book could only have been written by someone "well-acquainted" with grief. Long before Danny became the pastor standing by a casket at the front of the cemetery tent, he had been a "front-row" griever. And God, who as Pastor Goddard reminds us "comforts us in all our sorrows," used these deaths to shape a pastor's heart on the forge of reality.

I wish every pastor-to-be had to read this book before receiving a minister's license. I wish every new board member had to read this book. This book is that important for New Testament believers! We used to sing, "Give me that old time religion." Its lyrics, "It will do when I am dying" could be sung, "It will do when I am *grieving!*" especially if we change the *I* to *we*.

Too many grievers have been wounded in the most cr*itical* moments of grief by those who thought they could improve on compassionate silence and "deeds of love and kindness."

As you read this book ask the Spirit to touch your heart. It is easy to read these paragraphs and say, "Oh, I know someone who needs *this!*" But I think God wants to raise up grief-bearers through these pages. "God, what do you want to say to me through this pastor's heart?"

Each grief is a unique experience, even for those who have "frequent flyer miles" in the valley of the shadow. When it's Bob it's different than when it was Mary!

Dr. Mendell Taylor offered a nugget of wisdom to a college junior trying to sort out a call: "The God who had led you this far will not abandon you now." One sentence during a college revival has been pivotal in my ministry to the bereav*ing*. So, *when* "it" happens to you—and it will—what you have read here in these pages may be words the Spirit summons to the front of your heart.

With no sense of exaggeration, *What will we do without Bob?* are words "fitly spoken."

—Harold Ivan Smith, D.Min, FT

Introduction

Troubled

Let not your heart be troubled ...
(John 14:1, NKJV)

Tired and alone, I sat at a traffic light on historic Route 66 at Mustang Road in Yukon, Oklahoma. It was Wednesday night and I was on my way home from church. The radio was off, there was no CD playing, and neither was there any traffic noise that particular evening. I was just sitting in silence, a perfect opportunity for God to speak.

Suddenly, a strange question popped into my head: *"What will we do without Bob?"* For several seconds I pondered those words, words that obviously referred to my good friend, Bob Jung. In his absence, I had just prayed for Bob twenty minutes earlier in our midweek service and my plan was to visit in his home the very next day, evidently the reason he was on my mind.

But then, more thoughts came: *"We'll keep on listening to the music." "We'll keep on loving Jesus." "We'll keep laughing through life."* I realized the Lord was giving me a sermon—a funeral sermon—a funeral sermon for my friend, Bob.

My first reaction was: I didn't want to think about it. No one wants to go there. Many would say that Bob Jung was the life of our congregation. He was the organist and self-appointed jokester of First Church of the Nazarene in Yukon, Oklahoma. We've all heard that *Everybody Loves Raymond*, but I also knew that everyone loved Bob. Everyone. Oh, how we loved to hear Brother Jung play that organ on Sunday mornings. But our organ had been silenced since the cancer had returned. The only word most of the people heard about Bob was from the regular prayer updates given during the past few weeks in church. I drove home that evening and immediately typed those thoughts in a file on my laptop, hoping it would be a long time before the need to retrieve them.

The next day was Thursday, the day I drove the ten mile treck to Mustang for another wonderful visit with Bob Jung. Contrary to his usual self, Bob was quiet that day and mostly listened. Every now and then he would chime in with some witty remark as only Brother Jung could do. After we had prayed there in the bedroom, Bob's wife followed me to the door. Just earlier that morning, the hospice nurse had told her, "He's going down, but he's not going down fast." Kathryn insisted I go on to Kansas City for my two-week seminary module and they would be fine until I returned.

Monday morning came early and I flew to Kansas City. I grabbed my luggage at the baggage claim and caught the shuttle to the King Conference Center on the hill between Nazarene Theological Seminary and our denomination's former headquarters.

Having been in my room only about fifteen minutes, my cell phone rang. It was Kathryn Jung. "Pastor, Bob just passed away."

Talk about being hit with a ton of bricks! I was suddenly flooded with all kinds of emotions. I was shocked, I was sad, I felt helpless. I felt like I needed to run home as fast as I could. Instead, I did the next best thing: I prayed over the phone with Kathryn, then I stayed and waited. While I was away, my associate, Kent Mullens, did all the legwork for me. He met with the family, arranged the service, and tracked down those who would be part of the life's celebration. The funeral was planned for Friday, giving everyone opportunity to get in from out-of-town. I continued going to class that week, but in my spare moments I pondered that question, *"What will we do without Bob?"*

After my Thursday morning seminary session, I rented a car and drove to Oklahoma City. The service was to be at 2 p.m. on Friday, giving me all of Friday morning to finish my sermon which had been growing for days in my head. Up and at it early, the Holy Spirit helped me to bring it all together: *"What Will We Do Without Bob?" (1) We'll keep listening to the music. (2) We'll keep laughing through life. (3) We'll keep loving Jesus.* Those were the things Bob Jung did most of his seventy-eight years on earth and he did them well.

For some thirty-six months, Jesus of Nazareth had walked and talked with twelve chosen men and together, they had experienced plenty. Those disciples saw Him heal the sick. They witnessed His raising the dead. They were there when He fed the multitudes and they even stood with wind-blown hair, sopping wet in a boat, as He calmed the stormy sea. But now He was telling them that He was going away and no one wanted to hear it. As a matter of fact, the scripture says, "Peter took him aside and began to rebuke him. 'Never, Lord!' he said. 'This shall never happen to you!'" (Matthew 16:22) The Greek verb tenses tell us that once Jesus began to release this discouraging information, He continued to push it, and once Peter started rebuking Jesus, he also continued his reprimand. Observing from afar, we are appalled that Peter would argue with Christ, but we should never be so quick to judge. The disciples just could not imagine life without Jesus!

John tells us in his gospel that Jesus looked into the confused, frightened eyes of that ragtag bunch of followers and calmly, but deliberately, said, "Let not your heart be troubled." (John 14:1a) That word "troubled" is an interesting one, one that was used by John to describe Jesus Himself: "when Jesus saw her weeping, and the Jews who came with her weeping, He groaned in the spirit and was *troubled*." (John 11:33) "My soul is *troubled*, and what shall I say? 'Father, save Me from this hour'? But for this purpose I came to this hour." (John 12:27) "When Jesus had said these things, He was *troubled* in spirit, and testified and said, 'Most assuredly, I say to you, one of you will betray Me.'" (John 13:21) So a sister had lost her brother, Jesus was facing the Cross, and He was about to be betrayed by one of his own. These things "*troubled*" Jesus! (Italics mine)

The word "troubled" in John 14:1 means *"to stir or agitate"* much like water in a pot that has been brought to a rolling boil. It's a churning. It's an agitation. Most of us have felt that gut-wrenching churning deep within. In the Bible, as we go from version to version, we often find a word translated into several different words, but in checking eight different translations, I found this word was always the same, "*troubled.*" Apparently, it's the best word to convey the connotation the apostle had in mind.

On that dreaded Friday afternoon at Yukon First Church, I looked at a congregation that had even filled the overflow of the sanctuary and I admitted with them that we were all "*troubled*" over the loss of Bob Jung. His passing left us with such a feeling of uncertainty. After all, he had been around seventy-eight years. He was married to Kathryn for fifty-eight years. He had worked for the government over thirty-four years. He was the father to Beverly, Ron, and Don, and he had been a "fixture" to so many in the church. How does one walk away from that? Bob's gone and we were *"troubled!"*

After the committal service at a beautiful cemetery on the south side of Oklahoma City, the funeral director and I were discussing a book I had written that was soon to be published. *Pastoral Care in Times of Death and Dying* was primarily written for pastors and other caregivers, outlining in a very practical way the steps in ministering to the dying, conducting the funeral, and all that follows. Having overheard our conversation, a lady introduced herself as a journalist and explained how she writes for various publications. She complimented me on the sermon but then suggested that such a message is applicable for everyone. She pointed out how everyone at some point in their life loses a loved one and she thought the title was perfect, *What Will We Do Without Bob?* She then added, "Just as God spoke to you sitting at that red light, (something I had mentioned in the opening moments of my funeral message), I feel like God told me to tell you that you must write that book!" Wow. I've never had anyone say anything like that to me before. I thanked her and assured her that I would definitely give it some thought and prayer.

After keeping that promise for several days, I was unable to get away from the intriguing idea. So I visited with Kathryn Jung, obtained her approval, then decided that I would indeed write that book, *What Will We Do Without Bob?* For you, however, it may not be Bob, but rather Tom or Juanita or Paul or Marilyn. Perhaps it's Mom or Dad or a son or daughter. Maybe it was a best friend who was closer than a brother. What will we do? They are gone and we are left. How might we function? How will we cope?

What's going to happen to me? My prayer is that the Comforter, the Holy Spirit of God, will powerfully use the words of this book to encourage an aching heart and help someone, hopefully you, to continue to enjoy life's best even in your loss.

—Danny Goddard

CHAPTER ONE

What Will We Do Without Bob?

We'll Never Be the Same

O my son Absalom—my son, my son Absalom—
if only I had died in your place!
(2 Samuel 18:33, NKJV)

Only one of hundreds, I recently attended the memorial service of a ten-year old boy who had, without a doubt, impacted an entire community. The pastor began by verbally admitting the many emotions represented in that place—sadness, disappointment, confusion, hurt, even anger. For most of those present, these feelings were accompanied by a plethora of unanswered questions. Why him? Why now? Why cancer? Why didn't God heal him? Why weren't my prayers answered? Why did God allow this? Why not me, instead? Why at such a young age? Why? . . .

Losing a son or a daughter is always a parent's worst nightmare. It is no surprise that King David was highly emotional when the runner came with news that his son, Absalom, had been killed in battle. Weeping aloud, the king shouted out for all to hear, "O my son Absalom—my son, my son Absalom—If only I had died in your place!" (2 Samuel 18:33) It mattered not that David was a seasoned warrior. He had lost the boy he loved and the nation's leader was understandably distraught.

I can still recall the first time I felt such feelings. It was about third or fourth grade and I had lost my great grandmother. My parents picked me up early from school that day and together we went to a small Georgia funeral home somewhere near Atlanta. It could well have been the first funeral I had ever attended and I remember sobbing in the car with every painful thought that I would never ever see my great grandmother again. It felt oh so final.

A few years would pass and I would lose my great grandfather, then later, another great grandmother who was much closer than the first, since she actually lived with us, and then a distant uncle and an aunt. While still a child, I even had a same-aged cousin drown in a dairy lake at a church picnic. Through all these experiences, I learned that regardless of how close or how far removed the kin, there was always a great sense of loss.

None of them, however, even came close to what I felt when I was twenty years old and received the news while at work that my Mother had just unexpectedly passed away at home. She was only forty-nine. I had just talked with her that morning before leaving the house. Speeding home, I ran every red light between my workplace and my home place, some twenty minutes away. All the way home the reality would suddenly hit me over and over again. It was overwhelming. It was gut-wrenching. I remember feeling like something inside me had been ripped away, exposing such an excruciating, gaping hole that no one should ever have to bear. Two years later on a Sunday evening, I experienced it all over again when my fifty-four year old father suddenly died of diabetes and kidney disease in the presence of my brother and me.

You know what they say—"Time will heal." I'll agree that time does help, but I'm not so convinced about the "healing." I hurt over the loss of my parents five years later, and ten years later, and even fifteen. As a matter of fact, as I write these words, it has been over three decades and I still miss my Mom and Dad terribly. Just a couple of weeks ago, some good news came my way and my immediate reaction was to call my Dad. Then I realized—he's been gone thirty-some years, but it really does seem as if it was yesterday. Just tonight Sandie and I were riding in the car with our grown son. Tommy told us that he has been overwhelmed lately with thoughts of his maternal grandparents and though she has been gone several years, he has had a strong desire to call his Grandma and share some new events going on in his life.

Only a few months after my parents had died, someone told me, "Give it time—you'll get over it!" But the months passed and the years came and went and I didn't get over it. I'm now at the place where I have been without them longer than I was with them and still it hurts. I finally decided one day that I don't want to "get over it!" If someone meant the world to you, if you loved and cared for someone so strongly, why would you ever want to "get over" him or her? Harold Ivan Smith gives no options: "A griever will not get over a loss."[1] The bottom line is this: Someone we loved is gone and we'll never ever be the same—and that's okay. It's not what we ordered, nor is it what we wanted, but it's okay. It's like Elizabeth Harper Neeld said, "Our lives have changed, but without our permission."[2]

The world continues to change.

My Mom and Dad never saw a personal computer, much less a laptop like the one I use today. They didn't know about cell phones or iPods or DVDs. They had never heard of frequent flyer miles or weapons of mass destruction or worship wars or a flat-screen TV. The world that is so familiar to most of us was not the world in which they lived. Everything is now new and exciting and different and Paul and Marilyn Goddard have been completely left out. At times it seems cruel and so discourteous, but the world has unapologetically continued right on—without the presence or approval of my parents!

A pastor-friend and I once went to Atlanta from Indiana to attend a preachers' conference. Born and raised in that city, I assured Randy that I knew my way around town. Now I had been gone more than a dozen years and since I had relatively no family left, I seldom got back there. However, I guaranteed him that we would have no problem finding anything. After all, Atlanta was my home! I knew it like the back of my hand! Once we arrived on the interstate in "Hot-lanta," I made some startling new discoveries. There was now an interstate loop outside the loop! When I had left in 1976 to go to college in Nashville, the Omni, the home of the Atlanta Hawks, was still fairly new. Now I find that the Omni had been torn down to make room for the Georgia Dome! I promised my friend a hamburger at the world's largest drive-in, the Varsity, but the North Avenue exit that I had taken so many times as a teenager was now completely gone with no trace that it had ever existed! We finally got our lunch but we had to take Tenth Street to Spring Street and double-back to get there.

One night after the conference we were going to meet a few preachers for dessert at Underground Atlanta, part of the city that had been burned during the Civil War. It had been turned into a city beneath the city with several intersecting streets lined with bars, restaurants, and shops. Leaving around 11 p.m., we boarded a late night city monorail, and we began a conversation with the only other ones on the train, a young couple seated across from us. They had just gotten off work at one of the underground restaurants. Mentioning that I was Atlanta-born and raised, I told how I used to occasionally go to Underground Atlanta to dine at a certain eatery. I proudly mentioned the name of the restaurant but they had never heard of it. I told them about another place I used to go to, but again, it was foreign to them. Finally, I reminisced about some other establishment underneath the streets, but it, too, no longer existed. I felt like I was in the *Twilight Zone!* Then it dawned on me: All had changed without me and without my consent and there was no lasting indication that I had ever been there!

As sad as it sounds, the world will continue on without your Mom or Dad or even your child. As a matter of fact, people will mention them less and less until your loved ones are pretty much forgotten—except by you. There's nothing any of us can do to fix it, and yet all will be fine. A marker in some cemetery will acknowledge your loved ones, but you personally will always know they had been there. Thank God for the memories.

Life goes on.

When I was a little boy, my Dad would take me to the professional wrestling matches at the City Auditorium on Friday nights. Since Daddy was never fond of paying for parking, we always parked blocks away and walked the streets of downtown Atlanta to the arena. More than once he pointed out the light that burned brightly on top of Grady Memorial Hospital. He told me that when it burned a brilliant green, it meant a baby had been born, but when the light was an eerie red, someone in the city had passed away. I don't know how true that may have been but I do know my Dad seemed to believe it, and I don't know if Daddy even later remembered telling me that or not but it sure made an impression on a six-year old kid. Each time I hear a lullaby played over a hospital speaker system to announce a birth, I think of those lights on top of a hospital building in Atlanta.

Death will always be a part of life. My theology doesn't allow for children becoming angels if they die, nor do I hold to the idea that God takes someone from us because He needs them in heaven. No one will ever convince me that death is "God's will" and that He knows best. Death was never part of His creation. It was introduced by sin. It's ugly and intrusive and painful and whenever we hurt, so does our heavenly Father. Thank God, there are times when He intervenes and changes the circumstances, but many times He just allows nature to take its course, that is, for life to go on. And go on, it does . . .

I married a girl my Mom never knew. I became a preacher and my Dad would have been thrilled, had he known. Neither one of my parents was aware that I would one day wear glasses or go to Disney World or have a son or write a book. Sandie's Mom never saw Tommy graduate high school and her Dad never saw him graduate college. None of our parents attended his wedding. So many things happen in these lives that are racing toward the future and the faster we go, the farther away we get from "the good old days" we enjoyed with that one we so dearly loved.

Roll with the punches.

A prizefighter must learn a very valuable lesson. When his opponent lands a blow on his jaw, if he is rigid, stiff, and unmoving, he may get his jaw broken. The lesson to learn is to "roll with the punches." When a hard right comes your way, connecting on the left side of your face, you will want to turn with the punch toward your right and let his or her glove follow-through. You'll be less likely to sustain a worse injury if you learn to "roll with the punches."

How true that is in life. No one said life is fair. As a matter of fact, the truth is, life is not fair. Ask the Apostle Paul. Beaten, imprisoned, stoned, shipwrecked, robbed, and mistreated by strangers as well as by his own, he was left hungry and thirsty, he spent many sleepless nights, and he experienced both cold and nakedness. (2 Corinthians 11:23-28) Yet throughout all of his near-unbearable experiences, he kept an attitude that was positive: "For I am not ashamed of the gospel of Christ, for it is the power of God to salvation for everyone who believes . . ." (Romans 1:16) "I can do all things through Christ who strengthens me." (Philippians 4:13) "For I am already being poured out as a drink offering, and the time of my departure is at hand. I have fought the good fight, I have finished the race, I have kept the faith. Finally, there is laid up for me the crown of righteousness, which the Lord, the righteous Judge, will give to me on that Day, and not to me only but also to all who have loved His appearing." (2 Timothy 4:6-8)

Stephen was another totally devoted born-again believer. He was completely sold-out to Jesus, making quite a difference in the world of the early church. The scripture says of Stephen, he was "full of faith and power, did great wonders and signs among the people." (Acts 6:8) Surely God would continue to bless his life and not allow any harm to come to him. But instead, Stephen falls into terrible misfortune. Heartbreaking accusations are made. Stephen is arrested and dragged to a mock-court experience. Phony witnesses are compensated to lie about him in public. Even the church people are stirred against him. Stephen makes his defense but only makes matters worse.

The world was putting the squeeze on Stephen, but what do we see come out? It wasn't a bad attitude that emerged. It wasn't curse words or other foul language that made themselves known. Stephen had every reason to be down, discouraged, and dejected, yet the Bible says, "And all who sat in the council, looking steadfastly at him, saw his face as the face of an angel." (Acts 6:15) Stephen was so full of the Spirit of Christ that when the pressure was applied, Jesus came out!

Not only were Paul and Stephen treated unfairly, but so was Christ Himself. Jesus was falsely accused, beaten, spat upon, and even crucified on a cross. At one point His followers, His closest friends, all decided to leave Him. (Matthew 26:56) Our Lord was left completely alone. Nothing was fair for the Son of God and so life is not going to be fair for any of us either. We just have to learn to roll with the punches.

It's okay to miss your loved one.

As we enjoy various experiences in life, we find ourselves saying things like, "Terry sure would have enjoyed this!" or "Chren would have liked to have seen this!" We remember and reminisce and we laugh and cry. It's all pretty healthy. Many times our friends don't want to mention our loss because they're fearful of "setting us off!" I guess they are afraid we're going to burst into tears or completely lose control. Now we understand they do this to protect us because they care so much for us and don't want to make us hurt all over again. However, I think sometimes ignoring the loss hurts worse than anything that anyone could say. Someone who had experienced this firsthand described it to me as "the elephant in the room." If we could only see that it's actually therapeutic for a survivor to talk about their mate of fifty-some years . . . If we could just understand that it's healthy to allow them to live forever in our memories . . . Don't ever feel guilty for missing your Bob or your LeNora or your Gramps.

In his book, *God of the Valley,* Steve Griffiths lays it on the table—"Death is commonplace."[3] The loss of those close to us is something we will all experience sooner or later. Never again will we see them in this life. We'll never hold their hand or hug their neck or spend any time with them on this side of Glory. Yet those people live on in our hearts, in our memories, on a regular basis. Hardly a day goes by that I don't think about someone now gone. Such visions usually make me smile.

Everyone in the palace tiptoed around King David. He had lost his son, Absalom, and he was in mourning. His heart was broken. I think that is a fair representation of how we survivors all feel. Why not me, instead? It's so unfair! I'll never be the same! And that's all true, yet: The world continues to change. Life goes on. We have to roll with the punches. It's okay to miss your loved one. You and I will never ever be the same—it will be different, and yet it will be okay.

CHAPTER TWO

What Will We Do Without Bob?

We'll Keep Laughing Through Life

A joyful heart is good medicine,
but a broken spirit dries up the bones.
(Proverbs 17:22, NAS)

As I write today, it is late fall. Although it has been unseasonably warm, we did recently have a cold snap. It only lasted a few days; yet long enough to make a colorful world outside. Many of the leaves have fallen, probably prematurely due to the Oklahoma wind. It all represents death. The grass dies. Trees become dormant. Animals hibernate. Browns, oranges, and yellows make us think that something has come to an end. I look out my window and see a flaming red tree across the street. Soon winter will arrive and all the leaves will be off the limbs and on the ground, leaving only stark sticks that reach their skinny, bare branches toward God. Our world will slow down and will occasionally experience hardships.

Even the Apostle Paul urged Timothy, "Do your utmost to come before winter." (2 Timothy 4:21)

Although winter reminds us of death, most of us don't usually mope our way through December, January, and February. As a matter of fact, some of the most joyful times of the year take place during those winter months. At Christmastime, we sing and laugh and rejoice, especially noticing a "ho, ho, ho" everywhere we go. Everything is illuminated. The sound of bells fills the air. Twinkling lights decorate our houses and lawns. All is festive. Families get together. Gifts are exchanged. Parties take place throughout the entire month. There's tinsel, mistle toe, and egg nog. "Tis the season to be jolly!"

Then on New Year's Eve we stay up half the night celebrating a clean slate. We play games. We fellowship together. We kiss someone we love at midnight. We dance under a dropping ball at Times Square in New York City and we wish each other a Happy New Year. With genuine sincerity, we confess to one another what habit we plan to break and how much weight we are going to lose! It's time to look ahead and make for ourselves a better, more productive life.

In February we express our love for one another and give valentines to our friends but then we give one that's special to that one who is special. Roses. Candy. Gifts. We do it all with heartfelt emotion, warm fuzzies, and tickly goose bumps. It's almost as if we've forgotten that it's cold, lonely winter time. Some even take vacation days and plan a trip to the mountains where they ski and play outside in the snow. Or, like a former parishioner of ours who was fed up with winter went to the airport and said, "Fly me where it's warm!" Later that day, he called his Mom from sunny San Juan, Puerto Rico!

Unfortunately, someone has passed away. That's probably why you're reading this book. It's extremely painful and we will never

ever get over it. We must realize, however, that even in the winter time of our lives, life goes on. The sun will still rise tomorrow. Grief is something we have to deal with and as Harold Ivan Smith says, "Sometimes the only way through it—is through it."[4] It's a little like the Apostle James, when he says the only way to develop patience is to experience some difficult times (James 1:2-3). Don't ever pray for patience! That's like asking God to pile it on!

We are confident that our loved one would never want us dragging through life, depressed moment by moment, all because of our loss. My Dad knew his days were numbered and left a handwritten note among his papers of importance, a note that was shared in his funeral service: *"Tell the people not to mourn over me but to rejoice, for I've gone to be with Jesus."* I believe our departed would want us to enjoy life and to live it to the fullest. After all, Jesus Himself said He came to give life and to give it "more abundantly." (John 10:10) It is not my desire to merely exist. I intend to live that abundant life of which Jesus speaks.

Therefore it is a healthy endeavor to be joyful in our hearts. The wise writer of Proverbs says that "A joyful heart is good medicine." (Proverbs 17:22, NAS) Other translations use such adjectives as "cheerful" and "merry" to describe our hearts. That's the kind of heart the Apostle Paul possessed about A.D. 62 when he wrote his powerfully positive piece to the Philippians, one with the subject of joy being a major theme throughout the epistle. Though he writes from a prison cell, chained to Roman guards, possibly awaiting his own execution, robbed of his rights and freedom, he uses the word "joy" or its derivatives over nineteen times in four short chapters.[5] For this reason, Philippians has been called "the Epistle of Joy." In one of his most disheartening moments, the apostle writes:

"I thank my God upon every remembrance of you . . . always in every prayer of mine making request for you all with joy . . . in every way, whether in pretense or in truth, Christ is preached; and in this I rejoice, yes, and will rejoice . . . Yes, and if I am being poured out as a drink offering on the sacrifice and service of your faith, I am glad and rejoice with you all . . . Rejoice in the Lord always. Again I will say, rejoice! . . . I can do all things through Christ who strengthens me." (Philippians 1:3,4,18; 2:17; 4:4,13)

Encouraging statements such as these don't usually come from death row! This, however, is the kind of thing we hear from victorious Christians who have the joy of Jesus in their hearts. It has nothing to do with where they are or where they've been or what they're going through. It has everything to do with Who they know—Jesus! Living the Christian life is not about me, nor is it about us, but it's all about Him. In the midst of turmoil, pain, and even tragic loss, I can have the joy of Jesus in my heart.

My friend, Bob Jung, the inspiration for this book, was a giant who knew how to laugh, although he had that dry kind of humor. Everyone knows someone who possesses such. It's the kind of joking where he didn't laugh much himself, but left everyone around him in stitches. At his funeral I suggested that when Bob met St. Peter at the gates of Glory, Peter probably extended his hand as a gesture of welcome, only to have Bob take it, turn it over again and again and ask, "Is that clean?" The laughter in that service confirmed that each person present had at some time or another been on the receiving end of that particular Jung joke.

Bob Jung was a jokester. He liked having fun. And the last thing he would want would be for us to mourn his passing and especially to feel sorry for ourselves. For sure, we need to develop a positive attitude. We need to know how to rejoice. We need to know how to smile. We need to learn how to laugh our way through life. What does that mean?

It means we know how to have fun.

Unfortunately, there are lots of people in the world who don't have a clue as to how to do that. They have no idea how to laugh. They never enjoy a good hysterical cackle, much less experience any real knee-slappers. They're unfamiliar with just letting their hair down and having a hilarious time. I think that's so unfortunate. Everyone should laugh every day. As a matter of fact, in the movie, *The Bucket List,* one of the items listed on the register of things to do before one "kicks the bucket" is to "laugh until I cry." My wife has the right idea. Whether she gets a chance to read the daily newspaper or not, she really tries to at least look at the comics. A little daily dose of *Family Circus, Garfield,* and *Peanuts* will always do a heart good.

Bob, Pete, and Tom are three men who run the sound system in my church. They are notorious for queuing up a sound clip for just the "right moment." Once I was preaching about a personal experience on a bitter cold night. I was telling how the blustery wind was blowing and the snow was on the ground. Going on in much detail, I apparently told my story for a minute or two, at least long enough for those sound techs to find the right bite from their library. Suddenly, the sound of a rushing, mighty wind filled our sanctuary. I realize that's something that has been done before, but this time it wasn't from the Holy Spirit, it was from our "sound booth boys!" The place erupted with laughter. Even I paused in my preaching and laughed out loud. It's okay to laugh, even in church. As a matter of fact, some of the funniest things happen in church.

As I read my Bible, it seems to me that Jesus wants us to enjoy life, something that is sometimes hard for us to see because we often think of the Word as being so sacred and sober and serious. I believe God wants us to have fun and enjoy life. French philosopher and writer, Voltaire, once said, "God is a comedian, playing to an audience too afraid to laugh."[6]

Now I do acknowledge that there are appropriate times for sadness. The Bible even says that there is a time to cry (Ecclesiastes 3:4), but we're not supposed to be down in the dumps all the time. No one wants to be around people like that. I remember a pastor on a district where I once served who was the most pessimistic parson I had ever met. He was negative, always seeing the worst, always so somber and serious about everything. He was constantly knocking the denomination, putting down the leaders, and griping about his own church. The writer to the Hebrews warned them about a "root of bitterness" that can spring up within the borders of the best and defile a whole lot of people (Hebrews 12:15). I found myself avoiding my preacher-friend and the same will happen to us if we're always in the pits of depression. No one will want to be with us.

I pray that never happens to me. I want to keep a positive mindset. I want to be encouraging to others. I want to be Christlike. I want to laugh and have fun. After eleven wonderful years in Yukon, Oklahoma, Sandie and I recently accepted the call to pastor New Castle, Indiana First Church of the Nazarene, just east of Indianapolis. As we were driving the 800-mile trip, I told Sandie (I'm sure with excitement in my eyes), "I can start all over with all my jokes!" Having heard them for over three decades, she didn't appear to be very supportive.

But I have always enjoyed having fun. That's why my Abbott and Costello DVDs are among my most prized collection. That's why I turn on the TV and search for Andy Griffith or Laurel and

Hardy. A poster of the Three Stooges used to occupy a prominent place over my bed at Trevecca Nazarene College in Nashville, Tennessee. For four years I woke up to the inspiration of Moe, Larry, and Curly every morning of the world. I sure wish I knew what happened to that poster. When we got married, that poster disappeared, along with my green leisure suit. I love to have fun.

It means we laugh about the good times.

Memorial services are much too sad. Most always, I intentionally attempt to get people to laugh at a funeral. I try to sprinkle my sermon with a few humorous incidents that will get people to remember some of the great times they had enjoyed with the deceased. Now you understand, I don't make fun of the one who is gone, but just trigger everyone's thinking of some comical moments they will remember and run with in their own minds. It usually leaves them thinking, "Yeah, that was Dad . . ." Even years later, it's good to look back and laugh.

Our Aunt Gene was once a school teacher and eventually the librarian of one of our Nazarene colleges. In her retired years she would enjoy taking in a game of *Trivial Pursuit* with nieces and nephews at Christmastime. We would pick a card, read the question, take a shot at it, and finally announce the right answer. As we tried to move on to the next question, Aunt Gene would comment about the correct answer to the previous question, beginning with, "Now let me tell you why . . ." From her travels abroad and extensive reading over the years, she would go into great detail, explaining about the Amazon River or the pyramids of Egypt. We would all sit and wait for her to be finished with her impromptu school lesson and we have snickered about that for years, not only behind her back but even to her face. She would laugh right along with us. When she was 94 years old, I preached her funeral and the title of my message was, *"Now Let Me Tell You Why!"*

Something happened recently that made me ask my wife, "What would your Dad say about this?" She gave the obvious answer and we both had quite the laugh together. This is not being disrespectful. It's not ridiculing the one you loved. On the contrary, it is remembering who and how that person really was and laughing about days gone by. In my opinion, it is a healthy way of keeping our loved one alive in our hearts and minds.

It means we have joy in our hearts.

Our son, Tommy, seems to have been born with a joyful heart. Now in his twenties, he is an accomplished percussionist and has always had rhythm in his bones. One Sunday morning when he was about two years old, I was dressing him for church. We usually donned him in knickers with suspenders and a bowtie. I always called it his "Phineas Bresee outfit!" (Bresee was the founder of the Church of the Nazarene a hundred years ago.) That particular Sabbath morning, Tommy was sitting on his changing table and I took out his shiny black and white Sunday saddle oxfords. He immediately burst into tears! I asked him what was wrong, to which he replied, "These shoes do make me dance!" Once those shoes were tied-on, it seems our North Carolina hardwood floors made it impossible for him to resist doing a little toe-tapping with or without music! Sometimes we just can't help it and realize we must dance.

Some people are way too straight-laced. Perhaps we should all purchase a pair of saddle oxfords. Even David "danced before the Lord with all his might . . ." (2 Samuel 6:14) Yes, there are other times when we don't feel like dancing. Many reading these pages are in the midst of such a time at this very moment. Hopefully, however, the times for toe-tapping will outnumber those periods of sadness. E.E. Cummings once wisely said, "The most wasted of all days is one without laughter."[7] I pray that I'll never lose the laughter, that I'll always have a song in my heart. With everything within me, I must guard the joy of Jesus.

CHAPTER THREE

What Will We Do Without Bob?

We'll Keep Loving Jesus

> Jesus said to Simon Peter, "Simon, son of Jonah, do you love Me more than these?" He said to Him, "Yes, Lord; You know that I love You."
>
> (John 21:15, NKJV)

I didn't think I would ever see the day, but one of my associate pastors was recently escorted *out* of a hospital. He had been there that day in Indianapolis to pray with a man who was to receive a pacemaker. Our usual clergical custom is to pray with the patient before surgery, then wait with the family until the procedure is over. A pastor's presence is usually comforting and supportive to a concerned family but it is also a good thing should things go awry in the operating room. For this particular visit, however, the outbreak of the H1N1 flu had changed things. New rules only permitted a spouse to sit in the waiting room and though Pastor Rex was granted a few moments for prayer, he was then politely asked to leave the building. Sickness can be a very serious dilemma.

One of my favorite stories in the Gospels is the raising of Lazarus in John, chapter eleven. Each and every time I read the account, there seems to be more new truths that almost leap off the page. What a story . . .

Lazarus was a close friend of Jesus of Nazareth and one day he became extremely ill. We are not told what kind of sickness it was but we do know that various types of fevers were widespread in that part of the world, at that particular time, many of them life-threatening. Perhaps he even had whatever type of flu was common in that day. The important thing is that Lazarus was so sick that his sisters sent a messenger to find Jesus.

Jesus was not nearby that morning but was on the other side of the Jordan River. He was up to His elbows in ministry—multiplying lunches, casting out demons, baptizing believers, and oh yes, healing the sick, the reason for His summons. While in the middle of helping the multitudes, He was desperately needed in Judea, the very center of His opposition. Somewhat surprised that Jesus was considering a return trip, His disciples reminded Him that the Jews had wanted to stone Him the last time He was in town (John 11:8). They seriously questioned whether or not this would be a smart journey to make. Thomas even said to the disciples, "Let's just go and die with him!" (John 11:16) Yes, it would be, without a doubt, a dangerous place to visit, but Jesus was needed by His friends, Mary, Martha, and Lazarus. Therefore, He went.

Now as we read the scripture, we first get the impression that Jesus is not aware of the urgency of the request, for after He gets the news, He continues to do what He had been doing. He doesn't seem to get in a hurry and even stays "two more days in the place where He was." (John 11:6) Had it been you or me, we would have dropped everything and rushed to the place of our suffering friend. How many times have we hurried to the emergency room or nursing home or intensive care unit of the hospital? Such an emergency always takes precedence over everything else. Surely, our Lord knew that but He failed miserably to give that impression, especially to the loved ones of the sick. But as we read further, It is soon clear that Jesus really was very much aware of what was going on, for He even tells His disciples, before the word was official, that Lazarus was dead. (John 11:14)

In biblical days in the hot climate around Palestine, a deceased person's body was usually buried the same day of death. In addition, embalming practices and procedures were not the best, nothing like we have today, so it made sense not to drag a funeral out for very long. Such was the case for Lazarus. He died and was entombed, probably on the same afternoon. Jesus finally arrives, help has come—four days late! But wait—this, too, was part of His plan.

In that day there was a far eastern belief that when a person dies, his or her spirit would linger around the tomb in hopes of finding a way to re-enter the body. The tradition was that once four days had passed, any hint of resurrection was absolutely impossible. As William Barclay put it, "Lazarus was dead beyond recall."[8] Had Jesus come one, two, even three days earlier, the raising of Lazarus from the dead would have been no big deal. But Jesus waited four days. He waited until new life was utterly unattainable. He waited until all hope was gone forever. He waited. Then, before a crowd of wide-eyed Palestinians, Jesus raised Lazarus from the dead, clearly a miracle, proving the power of God over even the last enemy (1 Corinthians 15:26).

When we lost our Bob or our Maegan or our Mom or our Dad, we understand they are gone from us forever. We know we'll never walk in the park with him or bake cookies with her or take a trip together—ever again. Her life on this earth is over. His time on this planet is done. They are gone. We must realize, however, that after four days, after four years, after four decades, Jesus is still here! He is not going anywhere for He has promised to never ever leave us. (Hebrews 13:5) And because Jesus is still here, that means God is still with us.

Gregory Clapper has written a book, *When the World Breaks Your Heart*. In his book he encourages us: "The cross of Jesus tells us that God is here in all that we can go through as human beings. The cross tells us that God is here in our brokenness and pain, in our tears, in our lowliness, in our desolation. The cross of Jesus tells us that God is here.

"The empty tomb of Jesus tells us that God will continue to be with us."[9] In our grief, we are not alone. In our time of sorrow, He is with us.

On November 5, 1972 I knelt at an altar on a Sunday evening and began my journey with Jesus. I grew spiritually under the preaching of Pastor Bennett Dudney and I suppose I just assumed he would be there forever. Never had I entertained the thought of his leaving. Never will I forget, however, the morning when he resigned Atlanta First Church. It hit me hard. I had only been a Christian about three years and Dr. Dudney was the one who had believed in me, the one who had counseled me, the one who had even prayed through with me to be saved. He had baptized me, received me into church membership, and buried both of my parents. Now he was leaving us (I'm sure I felt more like he was leaving *me*!) to go to Switzerland to lead our denominational Bible College! As Pastor Dudney was resigning at the close of his morning message, the question immediately flashed in my mind, *"Now what am I going to do?"* But just as quickly as that thought had appeared, the next inspiration came: *"I'm just going to keep on loving Jesus!"*

With all the respect and sympathy I can muster up, I say this: Though we loved our loved one so very, very much, we are still to love God even more. Christ told His disciples, "He who loves father or mother more than Me is not worthy of Me. And he who loves son or daughter more than Me is not worthy of Me." (Matthew 10:37) Luke makes the language even more sobering: "If anyone comes to Me and does not *hate* (italics mine) his father and mother, wife and children, brothers and sisters, yes, and his own life also, he cannot be My disciple." (Luke 14:26) Is Jesus Christ, the One Who taught us to love, really suggesting we actually *hate* one another? Of course not.

We can all speak of people in our lives we love unconditionally. They can do no wrong to us. They can never turn us against them. For such, we would give our right arms! I personally know at least two people who gave the very personal gift of a kidney in order for another to live. At the same time, there are a few for whom we might even die. They could probably be counted on one hand. Jesus of Nazareth, well aware of our feelings for others, was saying that our love for God should be so great that, in comparison, our deepest feelings for the one we love the most in this world would appear to be hatred.

As fond as we are of our friends, we are not strictly here for them. As much as we love our relatives, we do not exist even for them. Though not a popular thought, we are not to be all about family. The one and only reason we are breathing today is to love and worship and serve and obey the One Who created us. The only reason we are here is to glorify the One Who gave His life for us. Pastor Rick Warren said it way: "The ultimate goal of the universe is to show the glory of God. It is the reason for everything that exists, including you."[10] The problem with the world is that it has come down to loving the creature rather than the Creator. (Romans 1:25)

As I write this morning, I look out my tenth floor hotel room window overlooking Orlando. The swimming pool below is beginning to be crowded with people for the day. I see families—moms, dads, little ones. They all seem to be having an enormous amount of fun. The tiny ones with inflatable wings run to the shallow end of the pool. Moms sit on their patio chairs with their eyes fixed on their children. Although I cannot hear from my vantage point, Dads appear to snore in the sunshine. They all seem to be enjoying their Florida vacation, loving the time they are spending with those they love. But the truth is, they should love God more.

All of this makes absolutely no sense to the unbeliever but for those of us who have surrendered our lives to Christ, we understand that He is to be supreme. Paul explains it this way: "You see, at just the right time, when we were still powerless, Christ died for the ungodly. Very rarely will anyone die for a righteous man, though for a good man someone might possibly dare to die. But God demonstrates his own love for us in this: While we were still sinners, Christ died for us." (Romans 5:6-8, NIV) Jesus has without a doubt earned the right to be first and foremost in our lives.

The Resurrected Jesus stood on the bank by the water and said to Peter, "Simon, son of Jonah, do you love Me more than these?" He said to Him, "Yes, Lord; You know that I love You." (John 21:15) We have no video account of that scene. We are not sure if Jesus pointed to the net and the boat and the catch of fish and meant, "Do you love Me more than *these . . . these things . . .* more than fishing?" Or perhaps Christ pointed to the other disciples and asked Peter, "Do you love Me more than *these . . . these people . . .* more than you love your friends and family?" Or maybe our Lord meant, "Do you love Me more than *these . . .* more than these others love me?" Each time Peter responded, it was with a different degree of love in the Greek, each one less than what Jesus was expecting. We must love Him supremely, more than anyone or anything.

Unfortunately, there are those who appear to lose everything when they lose a loved one. Their ambition is gone, as is their drive, even their reason for living has vanished. Some turn inward, becoming a recluse, divorcing themselves from society. Others have a perpetual pity party. I've seen people return to the emergency room over and over with the same diagnosis: grief syndrome. The love of their life is gone and therefore their own life is somewhat over. We recently said goodbye to a dear saint in the church, a precious lady in her nineties. At her funeral, we knelt beside the wheelchair and attempted to comfort her widower. Everyone in the church was thinking, *"He won't be far behind."* We received word during yesterday's morning worship service that he had just passed away. It had been all of three months.

The good news is, God does not want us to live in miserable mourning. God wants us to live with victory! Jesus said to His disciples, "I am the door. If anyone enters by Me, he will be saved, and will go in and out and find pasture. The thief does not come except to steal, and to kill, and to destroy. I have come that they may have life, and that they may have it more abundantly." (John 10:9-10) Jesus doesn't want us moping around day-in and day-out, filled with gloom and doom and despair. He wants us to live a healthy, holy, vibrant life that's filled with the joy of Jesus. That's why He sacrificed Himself. There is no other way to live to where we can be effective in building the Kingdom.

I have never pretended to be a spiritual superman or to know all the answers but I have made a crucial lifelong decision. When I face issues of life that I cannot understand, I'll keep on loving Jesus. As I watch friends and family members, those I love, struggle and go through crises of life, I'll continue to love Jesus. If God calls people home who mean the most to me, I'll never stop loving Jesus. Even when I stand at an open grave with questions in my mind that will remain forever, I will always love Jesus.

Over the several years I was his pastor, I watched Bob Jung go through a few disheartening situations. I saw him battle cancer the first time but He kept loving Jesus. I was aware of the "spells" he often had and the discouragement when the doctors had no answer, but he never blamed it on Jesus. I watched him as he played the organ for funeral after funeral, services for some of his best friends, but he never ceased loving his Savior. What an inspiring example of what it means to live for Christ.

My friend made an impact on me, but Jesus picked me out. My family members carried burdens for me, but Jesus carried my cross. My loved one seemed to live for me but Jesus died for me. So what will we do without Bob or Ashley or Brad or Ramona? What now, after Tim or Paula or Uncle Fincher? What's next after Mom or Dad, after that son or daughter? He's departed, she's not here, they're gone and it hurts! It's heart-wrenching! What are we going to do?

No matter what has happened, we can keep on loving Jesus because He keeps on loving us. He'll help us with the rest.

CHAPTER FOUR

What Will We Do Without Bob?

We'll Keep Listening to the Music

... at night his song is with me
(Psalm 42:8, ESV)

As previously mentioned, the great man who was the inspiration for this book was our church organist for nine years. Oh how he loved to play during Sunday worship. Never will I forget *"On the Jericho Road," "Jesus and Me,"* and other offertories that came from his fingertips—no, they came from his heart. He was always available to play for a seasonal cantata, a wedding, or a funeral and he even enjoyed playing next to my son, who was on the drums. Bob had a song in his heart that so effortlessly came out on his keyboard.

Organists are not plentiful in the average church congregation these days. Since our dear friend left us, our church organ has been all but silenced. Some people would say that the song has died, but that's the farthest thing from the truth. A very talented instrumentalist has gone on, one who had been most influential in the lives of so many people, but the good news is the song did not die with him. Hence the assignment: It's up to us to allow that song to live!

That's why we must keep listening to the music. This is what Bob or Alice or Mark or Becky would want us to do. As a matter of fact, this is what Jesus would have us do! Remember what He said? "Let not your heart be troubled." (John 14:1,27)

Whether it was an accident or an extended illness, we usually regard any death as a tragic event. Chaplain Gregory Clapper identifies a "tragedy" as "an event that should not have happened."[11] He then explained, "Jesus Christ acknowledged the reality of tragedy and went on with life. Tragedy neither drove him to despair nor did it elicit a long 'explanation.' Jesus simply lived the mystery of a grace-filled, loving life in the midst of tragedy and called his followers to do the same."[12] Like it or not, death is something we will all face sooner or later, hopefully later. Unfortunately, it is inevitable that we will say goodbye to some we love along the way.

So what do I mean by "keep listening to the music?"

1. *Let the song live on.*

H.B. London addressed the Nazarene pastors and spouses of the Southwest Oklahoma District in the evening banquet of our annual retreat. There in the Petroleum Club, thirty-five floors above a beautifully lighted Oklahoma City, Dr. London challenged us with words that are calligraphically displayed in his study: *"The dream never dies, just the dreamer."* He added, *"The song never dies, just the singer."*[13] It is so important that no matter what happens to us, no matter what comes our way, we must keep on keeping on.

Remember what the Apostle Paul wrote to the Corinthians? "We are hard pressed on every side, yet not crushed; we are perplexed, but not in despair; persecuted, but not forsaken; struck down, but not destroyed." (2 Corinthians 4:8-9) Paul is suggesting that we absolutely must develop a powerful resilience. We must become like the old inflatable punching bag-clown many of us had as a kid. We would bop Bozo in his big red nose and he would immediately go down, only to bounce right back for more! Why was Paul able to have such an outlook on life in the midst of calamity? It's because he had previously stated that "we have this treasure in earthen vessels, that the excellence of the power may be of God and not of us." (2 Corinthians 4:7) It's not about us, nor our misfortune, nor our heartache. It's not about sympathy or empathy or anything else. It's all about Him.

At twenty-two years of age, I sat next to my retired circuit-riding preacher-grandfather at the funeral of my Dad. Only fifty-four years old at his decease, Daddy's last few years had been an awful downhill battle with diabetes and kidney disease. Six hours a day on dialysis three days a week, Paul Goddard grew weaker by the week. He knew what the outcome would be and just as he prepared for his death, he also even prepared for his funeral.

Written in his own hand, Daddy left very clear instructions for his service which included congregational hymns: *"Have the people stand and sing all the verses."* One of the three hymns he had selected was *"Victory in Jesus."* The congregation stood, the instrumentalists played, and we all began to sing. My Dad had always liked to sing loudly so that's the way most of the people sang. Upon the first few words of that song, my grandfather patted me on my leg and exclaimed, "That's *MY* song!" He said it in a way that almost implied it couldn't be used for someone else. A few years later in that same funeral chapel, I was privileged to preach my granddad's funeral and we made sure that same song was used for him as well. You see, the song is not for only one—it's for all. Even as one who had been closely connected to music is gone, the song continues to play—in the church, in our minds, in our hearts.

2. Let the person live on.

Our minds are powerful creations. If we so choose, we can make our brains refrain from thinking about particular things or certain someones. When the thought of a person pops up, we have the amazing ability to stifle it, to push it aside, to forget it. Sometimes we do that when we think of a deceased friend or family member because we feel that the reflection is much too painful. We move on. Our friends don't often help us here. Many times when the one we had lost is merely mentioned, those around us attempt to change the subject. They, too, are fearful of the hurt and sadness that might be caused. The last thing we want to see, however, is our loved one forever forgotten. In my opinion, it is a healthy thing to remember and reminisce and to allow that person to live on in our thoughts and conversations. There are so many things we can do to keep her or him alive in our minds.

We can talk about them.

You might have to let your friends or family know up front that you're going to be okay talking about your friend or departed relative and that you're not going to "go off the deep end!" I still enjoy talking about my parents, especially telling my son about them. He never had the opportunity to know my dad and mom. Perhaps it's much easier to remember now than earlier, but even only weeks and months after their deaths, I *wanted* to talk about them. Feel free to recall the past, cry about the sad places, and laugh about the fun times. It's okay. If you feel you need permission, then I grant that to you.

We can look at pictures.

Break out the photo albums. Put on the home videos. Take a trip down memory lane and relive some of the days that are now history. Share these times with the younger ones, especially those who did not know Fred or Shirley.

On a recent trip to visit family in Alabama, a box of faded photographs was brought out of a closet. Sitting in a chair across from the couch, I watched as Uncle Guy presented picture after picture to my newly-married son and his bride. I was pleased with their interest in each photo and the questions that they sparked. I could also tell that it did something for our uncle, as he revisited days gone by and was able to share with an interested great nephew and niece.

The same experience can be enjoyed by each of us. You'll recall incidents and even conversations that seem like they just happened yesterday. Sure, tears are going to come, but so will laughter and a warm feeling about days gone by. It's not easy to forget while staring at a photograph.

We can do something in their memory.

The Gideons do the wonderful work of placing God's Word in hotels, hospitals, and even the hands of students and military personnel. Some may not be aware that the Gideons also have a special program for placing Bibles in someone's memory. You might want to make a donation to your church or favorite charity in his or her memory or consider starting a scholarship at some school or institution.

Lately, while stopped in traffic, I've noticed lots of "in memory of" decals on the rear windows of cars and pickup trucks. Motorists are carrying that precious memory with them everywhere they go. Reality TV shows about tattoo parlors have educated me to know that more and more people are getting tattoos to remember someone who has passed on. Many even have a lifelike artist's rendering forever inked into their skin. Window advertising may not be to your liking and you may not want to go to the extreme of body art, but have you ever thought of planting a tree in remembrance? A couple in our church occasionally plants a tree in honor of a bride and groom. Trees are also planted in memory of loved ones. There are so many ways to honor a person who is now gone.

We can visit their resting place.

Unfortunately, I seldom get to my hometown anymore, but whenever I go to Atlanta, I always make a little trip to Marietta's Georgia Memorial Park where the remains of my Mom and Dad were left. To me, it's special to be able to stand there for five minutes and think, reminisce, and thank God for my heritage. If your loved one is buried nearby, you have the opportunity to go more often. Memorial Day weekend is a good time to decorate their graves with flowers or wreaths. That's why some places in the deep South still call it "Decoration Day." At different times of the year such as Christmas or Mother's Day and Father's Day, we always tried to take flowers to the graves of Sandie's parents, that is, until we moved so far away. Whether you are accompanied by someone or you are alone, a trip to the cemetery every now and then is not a morbid idea.

I do think, however, that one can even take this little visit too far. When we previously pastored in Indiana, I had noticed a mausoleum that had been erected in a certain cemetery. Every time I was there to officiate a committal, I saw that mausoleum and the same car parked nearby. One day I asked an undertaker about this and he told me the story. A man buried his wife on that site and had that elaborate edifice constructed in her memory. Every day since, rain or shine, that man has visited the resting place of the woman he loved. He kept a folding chair out there and spent hours, mostly out of guilt for the way he had treated her. It was a very sad tribute. He was desperately trying to make up in her death for what he had lacked in her life. Well, obviously, this is the extreme. There is nothing wrong with visiting a grave and paying respect, but whether we do so or not, let's at least make sure we allow our loved one to live on in our hearts.

3. Let the survivor live on.

Sometimes it's easier to let the deceased live on than it is to for the survivor to do so. The survivor? That's you. It's me. Survivors are those who have been left behind. Though our loss leaves us with almost unbearable pain, it is imperative we continue on with our own lives.

I understand some people don't believe that's possible. They reason, "I can't make it without him! It will never be the same without her!" Or they may go as far as to admit, "I don't *want* to make it without him or her!" This is, by far, not a healthy attitude. I'll agree that it's hard. It's tough. I think I had already said that it's gut-wrenching. There will be days when you're not sure how you'll make it. Liz Cowen Fuhrman describes times of loss as "some of the greatest tests" of her faith.[14] But regardless of the pain that is experienced in the loss of someone special, we must individually hold on to our own personal will to live.

Things did not always go well for the disciples or the apostles in the days of the Bible. Paul and Silas were unfairly beaten and imprisoned, all because of their faith. The jailer was commanded to "keep them securely," (Acts 16:23) so he placed them in the "inner prison and fastened their feet in the stocks." (Acts 16:24) I really get excited over the outcome: "But at midnight Paul and Silas were praying and singing hymns to God, and the prisoners were listening to them." (Acts 16:25) Notice this happened "at midnight." Everything seems worse at midnight. It's in the night when it's dark and we're alone that everything comes down on top of us. It was during such time that Paul and Silas were singing hymns and praising God! They were experiencing revival! They were worshiping and celebrating and praising God in their darkest hour!

You and I can do the same! Yes, we lost someone very dear to us. The pain is excruciating. The loneliness is agonizing. The heartache is horrendous. Yet in the midst of our sorrow, at the "midnight" hour, we can still sing and rejoice and live. This is what the Psalmist means when he talks about having a "song in the night." (Psalm 42:8)

I am so grateful that the song of Bob Jung did not die with him. As a matter of fact, a few months before his passing, his children asked him to play the organ while they recorded his music. One day as I visited his bedside, I mentioned the fact that he was listening to some beautiful organ music. That's when I was informed that the music was that of Bob himself. A few of those taped selections were played as the specials of his funeral service. Yes,

Bob Jung, who had played the organ at so many funerals, even played at that of his own. The song never dies. The song lives on.

CHAPTER FIVE

What Will We Do Without Bob?

We'll Keep Counting on the Comforter

And I will pray the Father, and he shall give you another Comforter, that he may abide with you forever.
(John 14:16, KJV)

How many times have we heard someone say, "I don't know what I would do if I lost him?" "I don't know what I would do if she were gone." "If something ever happened to her or him, I would not be able to handle it." And so they worry and they fret over the inevitable. Day after day, they live their lives utterly in fear. When that time of sadness does arrive, however, Christians usually find that they are, in fact, surprisingly able to "handle it." This is attributed to two reasons.

1. The amazing sufficient grace of God

The grace of God is a popular subject in our churches. We've heard sermons preached on it and we've sung songs about it. His unmerited favor. Grace is that love and blessing that God bestows upon us even when it is so terribly undeserved.

Perhaps we had never thought about how the grace of God seems to come in various shapes and sizes. We are well aware of His *prevenient* grace, the grace that seeks us out and comes to us before salvation. We're familiar with His *saving* grace, how He forgives us of our sins no matter how unworthy we may be. Then there is His *sanctifying* grace that comes when we are ready to surrender everything, emptying ourselves of self, in order to be filled with His Spirit. Finally, we are all thankful for His *sustaining* grace, the grace that keeps us and helps us along our journey with Jesus, even when the trip becomes treacherous.

Now might I suggest a fifth grace, one with which many are not familiar? I like to call it *"God's amazing sufficient grace."* It's a mercy of God that cannot be obtained until the moment it is needed, which in this case, is the time of death. It's the grace to which Paul testified when his prayers were not answered the way he had wanted: "And He said to me, 'My grace is sufficient for you, for My strength is made perfect in weakness.' Therefore most gladly I will rather boast in my infirmities, that the power of Christ may rest upon me. Therefore I take pleasure in infirmities, in reproaches, in needs, in persecutions, in distresses, for Christ's sake. For when I am weak, then I am strong." (2 Corinthians 12:9-10)

Oh how we dread the day when a friend or loved one dies. We look toward it with fear and trembling, wondering how we will ever survive such a heart-breaking loss. But survive, we do. As Christians, we discover that when that moment does arrive, there is suddenly an awareness of the almost overwhelming Presence of

God. His presence is undeniable, providing that special grace, one that is never available until the instant it is needed. We usually describe this grace in terms of "not knowing where the strength has come from." I've personally witnessed this God-given gift displayed in the life of a young mother as she stood by the casket of her beautiful little three-year daughter. She was consoling others as they filed by, instead of their consoling her.

This amazing sufficient grace of God has an amazing way of coming suddenly upon those believers who have lost someone. Many times I have experienced it as I have said goodbye to close relatives and departed friends. I have also witnessed this grace coming upon those in the time of their own death. I offered to take my Dad to the hospital on that fateful Sunday night. Unlike other times when he had come to me almost in a panic, asking that I rush him to the emergency room, this time his calm reply was, "No, I'm not going to make it through the night." He turned the conversation toward the Sunday evening church service that he had missed. "What did Pastor Dudney preach on? Were there seekers at the altar? Was anyone saved?" He was noticeably pleased with my answers to his questions. Less than ten minutes later, my Dad was with Jesus.

2. The ministry of the Comforter

Though His followers did not understand why Jesus had to go, He assured His disciples that He would not leave them as orphans. (John 14:18) He loved them way too much to just bail on them. His promise was to send the "paraclete," Greek for "one who comes alongside."

Few will ever forget the 1992 Olympic Games in Barcelona, Spain when Derek Redmond was in the lead in the 400-meter race. Having undergone at least five surgeries on one of his legs,

Derek was only 175 meters from the finish when that leg could do no more. He collapsed on the track as the other runners sped past him. Derek was not a quitter, however, and though he knew his hope of winning was gone, he was determined to at least finish the race. Refusing to mount the stretcher that had been brought to him by medical personnel, Derek started to hobble down the track, each step more painful than the one before. By this time, his father, Jim Redmond, was making his way down from the bleachers, hopping a fence onto the track. As security guards chased from behind, Jim Redmond yelled to them, "That's my son out there and I'm going to help him!"[15]

Jim Redmond caught up with his boy, put his arm around him in support, and together they continued down the track, Dad and son. The race had already been won by another, but 65,000 fans stood and cheered and clapped and cried as Jim Redmond helped his son, Derek, get passed the finish line. That's a picture of the Holy Spirit, the Comforter, walking alongside you and me.

We established in the Introduction of this book that the disciples were "troubled," "agitated," "stirred," but not for long. Though Jesus was headed to a skull-like hill called Calvary, He knew He would be raised from the dead, He would spend a few special weeks with His friends, and then He would ascend into heaven. Shortly after His departure, He would send the Holy Spirit, the Helper, the Counselor, the Comforter, to minister to all of His followers, then as well as now.

1. The Comforter will never leave us.

"And I will pray the Father, and he shall give you another Comforter, that he may abide with you for ever." (John 14:16) I like the way *the Message* translates: "I will talk to the Father, and he'll provide you another Friend so that you will always have someone with you." Jesus knew His followers would need the abiding Presence of God Himself in their most difficult hour. Friends would leave them. Even Jesus would go away from them. But the Holy Spirit would be their permanent Paraclete. He would stay by their side and by ours through thick and thin.

The Lord Jesus knew firsthand how frightening it would be when we would suddenly find ourselves left all alone. As He was arrested in the garden and led away into the night, His disciples, His faithful friends, "all forsook Him and fled." (Mark 14:50) His three closest buddies couldn't even stay awake long enough to pray for Him. (Matthew 26:40) Jesus was unwavering that it would be different with us. That is quite obvious throughout the scriptures: "Yea, though I walk through the valley of the shadow of death, I will fear no evil; for You are with me; your rod and Your staff, they comfort me." (Psalm 23:4) "For He Himself has said, 'I will never leave you nor forsake you.'" (Hebrews 13:5) So what is this Paraclete, this Comforter, going to do for us?

2. The Comforter will teach and remind us.

"But the Comforter, which is the Holy Ghost, whom the Father will send in my name, he shall teach you all things, and bring all things to your remembrance, whatsoever I have said unto you." (John 14:26) Our Lord had spent three years training these religious leader wannabe's. They had learned some valuable lessons for life but so much is forgotten from a thirty-six month crash course. Christ promised that the Holy Spirit will not only teach them new things but will also remind them of things He had previously taught them. How many times do I reach back into my childhood VBS days and pull out a Bible verse or a song or a teacher's quote that might help me with whatever I'm facing?

Perhaps as one is anxious about the loneliness of the days ahead, a statement of Jesus might be reassuring: "But seek first the kingdom of God and His righteousness, and all these things shall be added to you." (Matthew 6:33) What "things" is He referring to? He's talking about what to eat, what to drink, what to wear, whatever were the concerns of those distressing disciples. If we will just learn to seek and keep God first in everything, He will take care of all the other needs. He wants to wipe away our worry list.

3. The Comforter will testify of Christ!

"But when the Comforter is come, whom I will send unto you from the Father, even the Spirit of truth, which proceedeth from the Father, he shall testify of me." (John 15:26, KJV) As we go through days without our departed friend or loved one, we will be reminded of all the wonderful things Jesus did while on this earth. The Holy Spirit reminds us of such wonderful deeds as well as the fact that Jesus can still do anything even now. Sometimes in very direct ways and at other times in more subtle ways, the Holy Spirit will remind us of the love of Jesus and the presence of Christ in our lives. It may be through the words of a song on the radio or the sight of a bird in the snow or the smile on the face of a child. It may be through that still, small voice within. Through whatever means He chooses, the Holy Spirit constantly brings up Jesus.

4. The Comforter will convict and convince.

"And when He has come, He will convict the world of sin, and of righteousness, and of judgment" (John 16:8, NKJ) The Holy Spirit convicts the sinner of sin in his or her life. Without His knocking on the heart's door, none of us can be saved. It is the ministry of the Spirit through His prevenient grace to "tug on our hearts" and give us the glorious opportunity to respond to that grace.

But the Holy Spirit does not stop there. He continues to minister to the believer, not by *convicting* but by *convincing*. He convinces the Christian of holy acts and attitudes that should be possessed by a child of the King. We should be loving. We should be tithing. We should be witnessing. We should be forgiving. We should be growing and maturing in the faith. The Spirit of God convicts the sinner of how the past has been lived, but convinces the believer of how life should be. For the believer who has suffered loss, the Comforter is forever convincing him or her that they can continue on, even though their hearts are forever broken.

5. The Comforter will be our Guide.

"However, when He, the Spirit of truth, has come, He will guide you into all truth; for He will not speak on His own authority, but whatever He hears He will speak; and He will tell you things to come." (John 16:13) At the time of death, a survivor is overwhelmed with difficult decisions, especially if prearrangements had not been made. What funeral home or mortuary? Which casket? Which suit or dress? When and where will the services be held and who will officiate? Burial or cremation? What cemetery? What would he or she want? What now? A pastor or minister will be of great help at such a lonely time, as will family and friends, but there is no help like that of the Spirit of God. He guides our thinking and helps us to make the best decision in every situation.

In his classic book, *A Shepherd Looks at Psalm 23*, W. Phillip Keller writes of the ministry of the Comforter: "During my wife's illness and after her death I could not get over the strength, solace, and serene outlook impaired to me virtually hour after hour by the presence of God's gracious Spirit Himself."[16] Though others will be in and out, the ministry of the Holy Spirit of God will be of continuous comfort. That's why He is referred to as "the Comforter." He is the Spirit of Jesus Himself and He is available to help us through our darkest days.

I recently sat down with a friend for a visit. He told of how God had spoken to him a few weeks earlier with almost a lightning bolt to get his attention and keep him from making a massive mistake. My friend immediately obeyed God and he testified how the Spirit now continues to lead, but in a quieter way, almost as if to just say, "Keep going in the direction you're headed—this is right."

You and I cannot make it through difficult days on our own, but with the presence of the Spirit of God in our lives, we can face anything. We can even cope with the loss of someone so dear to us.

CHAPTER SIX

What Will We Do Without Bob?

We'll Keep Shedding Some Tears

Jesus wept.
(John 11:35, NKJV)

Night has fallen over Orlando. Writing from a tenth floor hotel balcony overlooking Disney World's Magic Kingdom, I am enjoying a much needed vacation with Sandie. Our son, Tommy, has even flown in to make things complete. In the not very far distance I can see Cinderella's Castle illuminated in alternating pinks and blues and purples and greens. When a breeze blows my way, I can hear the sounds of laughter and music, as well as an occasional whistle from the train that circles the park. I know the lights on the water are from the ferry boats and I see the monorails and buses hurrying people back and forth. Disney World has become known as "the happiest place on earth." Wouldn't it be wonderful if we could live in that world continuously? What would we give for a place that is full of nothing but happiness and contentment year 'round? The real world that you and I know does hold many joyful moments but, unfortunately, it is also filled with pain, sadness, even death. On occasion our joy turns to sorrow and our laughter becomes tears.

It's somehow comforting to us to know that even our Lord and Savior wept outside the tomb of His good friend, Lazarus. I know I have already mentioned Lazarus in chapter 3, but it's such a good story, I'm going to revisit him. While Lazarus was very ill, they had called for Jesus of Nazareth, but instead of following the messenger back immediately, Jesus stayed a couple of more days on the other side of the Jordan. You'll remember how He was heavily involved in ministry, healing the sick, casting out demons, opening blinded eyes, baptizing believers. He could have quoted Nehemiah, "I am doing a great work, so that I cannot come down." (Nehemiah 6:3)

Now since Jesus did indeed care about His friend, He finally did come, but too late—in fact, four days too late. Lazarus was dead and gone, his body already entombed behind a heavy rock. What I failed to mention earlier is the fact that Mary and Martha, the two grieving sisters, were a bit perturbed with their friend, Jesus. "Lord, if You had been here, my brother would not have died," Martha and Mary both said to Him (John 11:21,32, NAS).

Now Jesus knew He was going to perform the miracle of raising Lazarus from the dead, yet the scripture tells us He still stood outside the crypt and wept. Knowing His friend would be walking out of that cave within moments, I don't believe Jesus wept over the loss of Lazarus, but rather over the broken hearts of two grieving sisters. Our hearts go out to people in their pain and so did the compassion of Christ.

I recently read an obituary in the newspaper that requested no one wear black to a particular funeral because it was to be a celebration of life. Black is a symbol for mourning, therefore most people wear black to services for the deceased. A black suit is almost a "uniform" for a pastor, since it is the appropriate attire for weddings, funerals, and services of ordination. When I was only weeks away from being ordained an elder in the Church of the Nazarene, Sandie and I went into a little men's wear shop in a small town in Nebraska, shopping for a black suit. The salesman explained how they never kept black suits on hand but one could be ordered. His reason: "No one wants a black suit except ministers and undertakers." I replied, "That's why I need one," but never told him which one of those applied.

In addition to the wearing of black, it's a common sight to see people wearing dark glasses to funerals, memorial services, and committals. I suppose we're trying to disguise our red, swollen eyes. We don't want anyone to see we've been crying. It's a personal thing. Yet Jesus teaches us that it is evidently permissible to weep over a loss that has greatly affected us. As a matter of fact, some think crying is healthy, even cleansing. There is a Jewish proverb that says, *"What soap is for the body, tears are for the soul."*[17]

Serving two summers as a youth pastor in Fort Lauderdale, Florida, I stayed in the home of a most wonderful family. We laughed together, played together, worshiped together, and learned together. At the end of that second stint, I loaded up my '65 Chevy Impala that I called "Elijah" (because it took great faith to drive), said my goodbyes, and left. Before I started my car, however, I realized I had forgotten something so I went back to the house, opened the front door, and walked in, as I had done so many times during the summer. To my surprise, the man of the house was standing alone in the kitchen, sobbing uncontrollably. I guess I never realized how much I had meant to him. My heart still breaks when I recall that sight. There wasn't even a death, but there was a parting. Evidently, tears are an expression not only of losing someone in death but even of a broken heart.

The opposite is also true. Sandie and I had such high hopes of being parents. It is so difficult when young pastors are continually asked by church members, *"When are you going to start a family?" "It's been a long time since we had a baby in the parsonage!" "What are you waiting for?"* Sometimes well-meaning people can be so cruel and not even realize it. Little did they know that most of the times we went to altars at campmeetings or district assemblies were to pour out our hearts to God in request of a child. After eight years, the doctors told us it would probably never happen.

I'll never forget that morning as I sat among the women in that gynecological waiting room, reading my book and working on a sermon for Sunday. The door opened and, of all people, **I** was called back. As I approached the door, I noticed tears in the eyes of the nurse. She opened the door wider and I saw another nurse and my wife standing in the hallway, crying. As I walked in, the doctor was coming down the hall from the other direction. He slowed down and before I could get it out myself, he asked what was wrong. The nurse managed to get the message out that we finally had a positive pregnancy! Sandie and I embraced and wept and the doctor even joined us! Those tears were tears of joy and now we have a married son, our "miracle," all grown up and working on his masters. Tears are a way to communicate our heartfelt feelings, good as well as bad. So Bob is gone. Nita has left us. Grampa will never be back. And it's okay to cry.

United Airlines Flight 232 had left Denver on July 19, 1989 and was headed for Chicago, but horribly crashed near Sioux City, Iowa. National Guard Chaplain Gregory S. Clapper was one of those who ministered to survivors and family members at the crash site. Upon viewing the bodies of a father and son with the Dad's arms wrapped around the boy, Chaplain Clapper broke down and cried. He later recalls, "As I stood there crying, a security policeman asked if I was okay. I said, 'Yes' and thanked him for his concern. I continued to cry. I could think of nothing more 'okay' to do."[18]

There will be days when your family is trying to do something fun and all you can do is cry—and that's okay. There will be moments when you're preparing dinner or working in the shop and suddenly the tears begin to flow—and that's perfectly alright. There may even be times when you'll be driving in your car and your view will be unexpectedly hindered by tears, so much that you'll pull over to the curb to sit and sob—and that's just fine.

I think sometimes the reason people don't bring up our loss is because they're afraid we're going to burst into tears on the spot and be completely out of control. But please understand, if you are a normal human being who loves and thinks and feels, then you'll have your moments, your "crying spells." No one else knows what or how you feel. No one else has experienced what you have been through. Perhaps they did lose a spouse, but they didn't lose *your* spouse! Maybe they did say goodbye to a child, but it wasn't *your* child. No one can know exactly through what you are going. These moments of tears will come and go for days, weeks, months, and years to come, and it's perfectly normal. Harold Ivan Smith says, *"Tears are a natural seasoning of the season."*[19]

My Dad owned a duplex three exits from downtown Atlanta, the house of my childhood. We lived on one side of that house and my maternal grandparents lived on the other. We called my Grandfather "Paw Paw." He was a good man. We were pastoring in Wilmington, North Carolina when we received the phone call from my brother-in-law that Paw Paw was gone. Sandie was expecting our son and was unable to travel, so I boarded a jet to Georgia alone and flew for awhile on what seemed like the loneliest flight in the world. I had a window seat and I buried my face against the double glass and quietly cried from Wilmington all the way to Atlanta. There were moments when I felt embarrassed, wondering if anyone noticed, if anyone wondered what was the matter with me. But no one seemed to see and all I could do was silently sob at 35,000 feet. I now realize it was okay.

I remember the story from one of our Nazarene churches of a man who had been murdered, leaving behind a young wife and children. The widow seemed to keep it together until she started going through his clothes. She had taken several suits from her husband's closet when it suddenly hit her, again. Clutching those suits to herself, she slid down the closet door to the floor, and she sat there and cried.

A lady in a church we pastored had lost her husband in a tragic accident. I'll never forget the sight, weeks later, when two people led her, almost carried her, into my study during the Sunday School hour. She was weeping uncontrollably as the reality had sunk in, one more time. This scene was repeated again and again over the next few months. I can say that I personally understand. One may go weeks, even months after a loss and then seem to say, "Alright, it's now been ten months. That's long enough. I now want my Dad back." "It's been two years and it's now time for Mom to come home." But they're not coming back. Any loss is hard to get through, but especially when the person is young and the event is so tragic.

The young couple seemed like kids themselves but had just lost their six-year old boy in a drowning accident. Being their pastors, Sandie and I were with them at the funeral home, trying to help them make arrangements, but all they could do was cry. They finally asked us to do them the favor of finishing the morbid task, so my wife and I selected a powder blue casket and made other decisions before getting their final approval. They certainly had a right to shed tears then and for many years to come.

Sometimes we get the idea that tears are signs of weakness, especially if you happen to be a man. It's supposed to be the lack of masculinity. But tears are not a sign of anything except that of your loss. Tears are a language in themselves: In crying, we acknowledge our lack of control, our inability to have things the way we want them. In crying, we are not failing to be strong; we are being strong enough to acknowledge our weakness, our humanness . . . tears are the bodily expression of humility. Tears are our humble acknowledgement that while we are beings created by God in God's image, we definitely are not God.[20]

For fourteen-and-a-half years, Bingo had been such a loving part of our family. Tommy's fifth birthday gift, that black lab had such personality that he was quite often an illustration in my sermons. We had so much fun with Bingo. Just a bit skittish, our "watchdog" once jumped onto the couch when we had a mouse in the house! When we moved from Muncie, Indiana to Oklahoma, he was afraid to lie down in the car and he stood in the back seat all the way to Indianapolis before he finally collapsed from exhaustion. Whenever there was a storm in the night, Bingo would jump onto our comforter and tremble until we thought someone had put a quarter in the bed! Then he grew old. Arthritis took its toll. We could look into his eyes and Bingo was still there, but it was a cruel sight to see him drag his hind legs those last few days.

Sandie, Tommy, and I, his family, held him on the vet's table and we all told him how much we loved him and we all petted him and we all sobbed as his life was quickly taken away. Some would say, *"But that was just a dog!"* And that's true, but he was *our* dog, and it hurt. Tears are the only way we can express how we truly feel. The veterinarian's nurse stood nearby, misty-eyed. The doctor tried his best to remain emotionless and assured us more than once that we were doing the "right" thing, though at the time it didn't feel very "right." And it doesn't feel "right" when we lose the one we love the most—a son, a daughter, a husband, a wife. God has given us a way of release, a way to express our innermost feelings—tears. Keep a box of tissues close by if you must. And it's okay.

CHAPTER SEVEN

What Will We Do Without Bob?

We'll Keep Facing the Holidays

His peace will keep your thoughts and your hearts quiet
and at rest as you trust in Christ Jesus.
(Philippians 4:7, TLB)

My Mom was right (Moms are always right.). She told me that as I get older, time will fly by. When I was a kid, it seemed like each Christmas took three years to get here! Now that I'm older, it seems that we just get through the special times of the year and then, before you know it, it's time to start all over again. These days we see the department stores going all out for Halloween, only to go straight into Christmastime. I was in Wal-Mart this year on October 31 and noticed the girl was taking down the scary costumes and replacing them with Christmas ornaments. (Whatever happened to Thanksgiving?)

They're upon us again—the holidays. They're always upon us. As I write this morning, we're only a week away from turkey day. Soon we'll be part of a crowded mall with music playing and lights twinkling and people rushing. They'll hurry around for hours with arm-loads of packages and shopping bags. They will have one thing on their minds: Finding that perfect gift for that perfect person. You and I will also have someone on our minds. We'll be thinking of Dad or Mom or Gwen or Jimmy, the friend or family member we have lost.

Please understand, it's not that we're a bunch of Scrooges or a group of grinches out to destroy the season. It's just not easy to get into the spirit of things when you're all alone or at least missing someone you loved. We've been wounded. It continues to hurt. Our loss is still new. She should be celebrating next to me. He should be shopping with me. It's so hard to join in the festivities and go on like my loved one never existed.

The holidays personally affect me just as they do millions of others who have suffered loss. My forty-nine year old Mom had opened her Christmas gifts but never had an opportunity to enjoy them. With no one aware of the cancer, she died suddenly on December 27. Christmastime was her favorite, and oh, how she loved a Christmas tree. She even loved that shiny aluminum one we had in the early sixties, the one with the color wheel that changed the entire wall of the living room from off-white to red, then green, then blue, then yellow, then red again. It was quite the light show that was visible even from the street. Sitting for hours at a time, Mama would stare at that Christmas tree as if she was lost in another world. At her funeral, Pastor Bennett Dudney mentioned her love for the Christmas lights and how in them she saw the Light of the world, Jesus Christ.

Almost two years to the day, my family was back at the same funeral home. This time my fifty-four year old Dad was not with us to make the arrangements. They were for him. His Christmas gifts were also opened but stacked neatly in his room. Now you must understand, I am reaching back thirty years, yet I cannot go through a Christmas season without thinking of the deaths of my parents. Those two traumatic events have become permanent parts of my Advent season.

There are now some fresher thoughts during the holidays—recollections of my mother and father-in-law who have more recently passed away. Thoughts of their deaths are extremely difficult because it was just a few years ago when they were both vibrant parts of our family celebration. Part of the laughter we heard was theirs. Tom was one of the men snoozing in the recliner during the football game. Juanita was always in the kitchen, making sure everything was just right. We now do it all without their physical presence, and it's tough.

Especially difficult are the "firsts" that come along after one's passing—the first Thanksgiving, the first Christmas, the first anniversary, the first wedding. As a pastor, I keep track of deaths in our congregational families, categorizing them by months of the year. Each month my administrative assistant provides for me a "bereavement list," listing the name of the family, the name of the deceased, the kinship, and the date of death. (When I started this ministry, I called it "Death List," but decided it may fall into the wrong hands, someone who may not understand!) I send a letter of encouragement to that family on the first few anniversaries of their loss. Most people forget the date or even the time of year someone dies. Life goes on and so do they. The griever, however, never forgets. The mourner lives every day with the thought of their loved one's departure foremost on their minds and every single day that mourner hurts.

We used to have such a huge family gathering during the holidays but now we watch our crowd grow smaller year by year. As we were driving to our Cousin Nita's house for Thanksgiving, I counted in my mind ten people now missing from around our table. The Associated Press printed an article in the newspaper on Thanksgiving Day that addressed this. The article talked about a lady in Minnesota who lost her father in the collapse of the Minneapolis bridge, another woman whose husband is entombed inside the Crandall County mine in Utah, and a family that mourns the tragic death of their 20-year old college student in the Virginia Tech shootings. But all of these people will make it through the holidays this year and next and the next:

> "Those left to press on have found strength in friends and family, and have discovered strength of their own to share with others. They're thankful for something else, too: loving memories of the people they mourn."[21]

With that in mind, I'd like to share a few thoughts concerning holidays ...

1. It's okay to enjoy the holiday without your loved one.

One thing we cannot do is stop the holidays from coming. Helen Fitzgerald explains, "No matter what your religion may be, Christmas is all around you, coming at you from all directions."[22] Like it or not, Macy's is still going to have a parade, Rudolph's red nose is still going to glow, and Jimmy Stewart is still going to realize it's *A Wonderful Life*. If we choose to refrain from participating in the merriment, it will just take place all around us.

My son played drums in a jazz combo at Southern Nazarene University in Bethany, Oklahoma. Now that he's in graduate school, it has become harder for the group to get together, but they do occasionally give it a try. *Asbury Lane* once played five gigs at Oklahoma City's Penn Square Mall during the Christmas season, playing yuletide music for two hours at a time. As I sat there listening to Tommy and his friends present the sounds of the season, I watched people. They came into the mall entrance only several yards away and once they heard the music, smiles broke out across their faces. Some even literally danced by. Many stopped and listened. Children stared and pointed. One couple stood and swayed with the music. It made me feel good that these young men were bringing some holiday cheer into the lives of stressed-out shoppers.

But then I saw one gray-haired woman come in from the cold. She approached the combo from behind and as a grimace took over her face, she literally covered both ears with her mittened hands. She walked past the melodies and into Dillard's department store, holding her ears tightly until she was out of sight. I wondered about her story. The impression I got was that no one was going to force Christmas on her! Joy and cheer was not about to enter her mind! Sadly, this is the outlook of many grievers as they face the seasons of celebration.

I really think if we took the time to consider it, we would each come to the realization that Mom or Dad would not want us moping around while everyone else is having a grand time. That is especially true if the departed one was really into the holidays. Some grievers go as far as refusing to send Christmas cards, put up a tree, or join in on any of the festivities.

Nothing is accomplished by our failure to party. The only thing it does is feed a "poor-me" attitude. We watch the fun from afar and feel sorry for ourselves. Let us remember that Thanksgiving, Christmas, and Easter are not about us or even them—it's all about Him. At Thanksgiving we express our genuine gratefulness to God for His many blessings. During Christmas, we celebrate the Birth of Jesus, Who was born to die for each of us individually and set us free from the grip of sin. Then on Easter Sunday, we get excited about the Resurrection of Christ which makes our hope a reality. Our departed friends may have been all about the holidays, but the holidays were never all about them.

There's an empty chair at the Thanksgiving table and there are fewer presents under the tree. We remember and we hurt but we join in on the celebration because of our love and devotion for Him. God is not to blame for our times of sadness. His Heart breaks right along with ours and He weeps whenever we weep.

2. It's okay to include the departed in your celebration.

Aunt Sarah or Uncle Charles will not be with us physically this season but they will be with us mentally and emotionally. Why not include them during this holiday time? Pull out Juanita's favorite cornbread dressing recipe for Thanksgiving. She's not around to personally prepare it anymore but you can pick up the baton and keep the tradition going. It's like making it in her memory. Perhaps Tom hung the Christmas lights on the eaves of the house a certain way. Now is the time for you to add that to your list of decorating tasks. Do it the same way Tom would have done it. Maybe no one else will notice, but you will, and you'll smile as you remember.

When we were first married, Sandie and I started a Christmas tradition that has continued to this day. We purchase a single Hallmark Christmas ornament that displays the date of that particular year. We also search diligently to find one that commemorates something that was meaningful for that year. A couple of our ornaments depict a trip to Disney World or when my in-laws travelled the miles to pay us a visit. We have one reminding us of the year we added Bingo to our family and one for the birth of our baby. Why not get an ornament to remember your friend or loved one in some tasteful way and hang it on your tree, not only this year but all the years to come. As a matter of fact, we usually have a formal Christmas tree in the living room but we have another tree in the family room that is adorned with all those special decorations of remembrance. Shortly after a loss is a good time to start new traditions.

3. *It's okay to shed a tear amidst the festivities.*

I think it's a healthy thing to remember and reminisce about days gone by.

The holiday season usually triggers some hilarious anecdote about the one who is gone. *"Remember when Uncle Elmer used to play Santa Clause down at the shopping center?" "I'll never forget when you were making chocolate balls for our Christmas parsonage open house and your Dad didn't know they were frozen until he threw one up to catch it in his mouth and almost broke a tooth!" "There was never a Christmas when Daddy didn't bring a fruitcake and eggnog home from work!"* Thus we include our departed ones by remembering them in our holiday sharing times. In this way, they can live on.

But it's okay to do a little crying during the holiday season, as well. You might want to visit a gravesite and leave a poinsettia. I have even seen a few small decorated Christmas trees standing on graves where that is permissible. Some funeral homes now have annual memorial services where you can light a candle in memory of the one you loved. I have been privileged to speak at two of those for two different funeral homes during the past two Christmases. You may shed some tears during the season and that's perfectly alright and even expected. Just don't become a recluse. Don't turn inward and away from those who love you. Don't replace the Christmas party with a personal pity party. That's when actions cease from being healthy.

Thanksgiving time is a good time to express to God our gratitude for that one or those ones who had so significantly touched our lives. Thank God, it wasn't a death, but our only son was married in the summer of 2010 and we had to begin this "sharing thing" during the holidays. We were going to have Tommy and Micha home in Indiana for Christmas but they would be at her parents' table in Tulsa for Thanksgiving. What were we going to do? For the past twenty-some Thanksgivings, the three of us were together! What in the world would we do? ...

I'll tell you what we did—we flew to Disney World! Just the two of us. Sure, we missed both Tommy and Micha, but Sandie and I had a wonderful time! We had Thanksgiving dinner at Magic Kingdom's Crystal Palace, where every fifteen minutes or so, Winnie the Pooh, Tiger, and other characters led the children around the restaurant in a five-minute "pooh-rade!" We knew we needed a mighty big distraction to make it through the holiday so we opted for a Florida vacation. Perhaps that's what you need to do to get on the other side of that first Thanksgiving or Christmas. It may not be Orlando for you, but get out of town, plan a trip that is sure to be fun. Oh, you'll miss your loved one and you'll have your tearful moments, but do whatever is necessary to make it through those initial celebrations without him or her.

As life goes on, we must continue to face up to the future and that includes facing the holidays with our loss. Again, this is where that "amazing sufficient grace of God" comes in for this is one of those tasks that is much too difficult to do ourselves, alone, on our own power. Paul said, "I can do all things through Christ who strengthens me." (Philippians 4:13) If we call upon Him,

He'll help us enjoy the big celebrations throughout the year and we don't have to betray the deceased to do so. Let's celebrate and remember.

CHAPTER EIGHT

What Will We Do Without Bob?

We'll Keep Thanking God

> "in everything give thanks; for this is the will
> of God in Christ Jesus for you."
> (1 Thessalonians 5:18, NKJV)

Looking out my hotel window this morning, I see huge green pine trees reaching into the blue sky. My wife and I are in the foothills of the Appalachians in North Georgia on our way home from a Florida vacation. Yesterday we hit Atlanta at traffic time. I guess I should specify, since most times in Atlanta are traffic times. To be more specific, it was the rush hour, around 6 p.m. We were in bumper-to-bumper traffic thirty miles south before we ever hit the city! It didn't really bother me since Atlanta is my home, or I should say, my hometown. Although the place has grown without me, I grew up with daily transportation at a crawl. I will admit, however, that there is much more of it today than there was yesterday. Atlanta, Georgia has always been a busy place.

While in Atlanta, we made our way to downtown and, of course, to the Varsity, the world's largest drive-in, to which I have already alluded. I had to have my regular order of two hamburgers, fries, a fried peach pie, and a Coke (Well, that has changed over time to a Diet Coke). This sure sounds good at the moment. There are now years between my orders but when I was a kid, this was my regular Thursday night meal. My Dad worked fulltime for the downtown Atlanta Post Office but drove a Brinks truck part time a couple of days a week. Every Thursday of the world he went to Lockheed in Marietta to cash paychecks for the airplane builders. On his way home every Thursday night he stopped by the Varsity and brought home our supper.

After yesterday's Varsity visit, we headed up I-75 toward Indiana, but made a very important stop before getting too far away. Located on Windy Hill Road in Marietta is Georgia Memorial Park, a beautiful perpetual care cemetery with its own funeral home. Striking statues of Jesus in different scenes of His ministry divide the burial grounds into sections, making it a bit easier to find a particular resting place. We drove around to the left and found a shady place to park on the street near the end of the walkway. We walked up the sidewalk that led us to two graves, those of my Mom and Dad.

Sandie and I stood there and talked. We talked about how it is unbelievable that they have been gone thirty-some years. "It's just like it was yesterday," I told her. We talked about the fact that she never knew my Mom but did know my Dad for about a year or so. That conversation led to one about Tom and Juanita, my in-laws. They, too, are dearly missed by both of us. After spending a few moments there, we left and I think we were both silently thanking God for wonderful parents. Only God knows when I'll get by there in the future.

One thing we can never do is see our loved ones again on this side of Glory but we can still thank God for their influence on our lives. We will never be able to talk with them again but we can be grateful for the memories that seem to keep them close. We cannot hear their laughter or experience their concern or watch them do whatever they did best, but we can reminisce and remember and recall, all the while thanking our heavenly Father for the time we had together.

The attitude of gratitude is an extremely crucial characteristic of the Christian. Jesus healed ten lepers one day and only one returned to thank Him. We can almost feel His disappointment as He asks the one, "Where are the nine?" (Luke 17:17) Thanksgiving was evidently expected by Christ then and I believe He still expects it today. Giving thanks should be a regular part of our daily lives. Dr. Stan Toler calls it "a heart habit."[23] In his book, *Total Quality Life,* he even shares the results of clinical studies that have proven the attitude of gratitude plays a significant role in the overall well-being of a person. A thankful person is one who is more alert, more enthusiastic, more determined, more optimistic, and greatly energized.[24]

I realize when one is in mourning it is not an easy task to feel very grateful. It's almost like the lights have gone out and you've been left in the dark—alone. And there is no set amount of time for grieving. It may be ten weeks or ten years. For some, it's a lifetime. But regardless of how we may feel at the moment, I believe if we sat down for a few minutes to think, we would come up with numerous reasons to praise God. For example ...

Thank God for our heritage.

Recently, on a Wednesday evening, I was telling my congregation that, had it not been for my heritage, I don't know where I would be today. Raised in church, I am a third generation Nazarene. My grandpa was a circuit-rider preacher. He preached in three Methodist Churches that alternated on Sundays. My Dad was a powerful layman who made sure Harold, Vickie, and I were in our seats in Sunday School each and every Sunday.

I remember those Sunday mornings when either Harold or I (and sometimes both of us) would decide we "weren't feeling very well" and should probably stay home from Sunday School. Daddy would come into our room and find us laughing at the comics from the morning newspaper, a Sunday morning ritual. He would quietly but firmly "convince" us that we needed to get ready for church. At the Goddard house, it was more plausible to miss public school before missing Sunday School. Church and Sunday School were pretty high on my parents' list of priorities.

Moses passed the words of God about the Word of God to the Israelites:

> "Keep these words that I am commanding you today in your heart. Recite them to your children and talk about them when you are at home and when you are away, when you lie down and when you rise. Bind them as a sign on your hand, fix them as an emblem on your forehead, and write them on the doorposts of your house and on your gates." (Deuteronomy 6:6-9, NRSV)

That's pretty much the way it was at our house. The Old English *"Prayer Changes Things"* plaque hung forever on that living room wall. Whether we were working or playing, Daddy always took five minutes to sit on a rock, pull me onto his lap, and tell me how Jesus wants me to live. Even if away on vacation, we knew we would be back on Saturday night because we did not dare miss Sunday School on Sunday morning. That's my heritage and I hope one that's similar is yours.

Perhaps that is not the way you were raised. As a matter of fact, it may look nothing like your childhood days. God is always about doing new things (Isaiah 42:9) and there is no better time than the present to commit your family to Him, creating a heritage for those who will follow you. Thank God for a godly heritage.

Thank God for life's lessons.

I sat on my Mom's lap when I was, as Brother Chilton used to say in the old Atlanta First Church, "just a pup," and she would tell me about Jesus. My Dad taught me to tithe and that church is important. From my parents, I learned about faith, reading my Bible, how to pray. I also learned how to treat people in the same way I would want to be treated.

Like my Dad, I love watermelon—love it! For whatever reason, my Mom believed that you could not eat watermelon until after the Fourth of July. If you did, you would get sick. To this day, I don't eat watermelon until after Independence Day! I remember once as a little boy becoming irritated over all those "millions" of seeds in a watermelon! I became so weary of having to pick out all the black ones, the brown ones, and those tiny white ones. I just wanted to dig in and eat it. One day I asked my Dad, "Why doesn't the man at the grocery store pick the seeds out of the watermelon before we buy it?" My wise Dad answered my question with a question, teaching me a powerful lesson: "Son, would you want someone going through your watermelon before you eat it?" That answer has seemed to suffice for all these years.

Well, that was but one lesson for life from my father that I still remember to this day. No doubt, we have learned so many things from our now departed friend or loved one. Though he or she is no longer around, the lessons we have learned are with us forever. Thank God for the lessons of life.

Thank God for our memories.

Recently I officiated the funeral for a longtime member of my church. It was held in the chapel of the funeral home and the service and final viewing were over. The family had left the chapel, the doors had been closed. The funeral director was making the final touches—removing the watch and rings, cranking the body down into the casket, adjusting the lining so the lid could be closed. That's when he noticed her—a daughter and her husband were standing not ten yards away, watching every move made around her departed Dad.

I saw the mortician hesitate. He thought all the family was waiting in the hallway. No one wants to see the casket closed on their Dad for the last time. Then I saw something I had never witnessed before. The funeral director walked over to the lady and very quietly asked, "Do you want to tuck him in?" She nodded and he led her back to the casket, showed her how to grab the end of the satin blanket and pull it up to her father's chin. After doing the very final thing she could do for her parent, she and her husband slowly turned and walked away.

I later related this scene to my son, Tommy, who responded, "She'll remember that for the rest of her life." And that she will. She will also always be thankful for her Dad and for the chance to do something special for him one last time.

Not long ago I was called by a local funeral home and asked to preach a funeral for an eighty-some year old man who had been without a pastor. I phoned the grown daughter of the deceased to gather information and later sought God for a message that was both personal and of comfort. Upon arriving at the mortuary just before the funeral was to begin, I introduced myself to the family. The daughter then said to me, "I want you to meet my father." I remember thinking, *"Am I not officiating the funeral of her father?"* Before I could ask any questions, she took me by the hand, led me to the casket, looked down at the deceased, and very politely said, "Daddy, this is Rev. Goddard." She then looked at me, as if I was to respond. I was speechless. Thinking quickly, I noticed a lapel pin of some sort on his suit coat about which I made some comment.

As I thought about that moment a little later, it dawned on me that this was a woman who had refused to live in the past. She was not going to think of her father in terms of how things used to be. She had chosen to not picture him as dead and gone forever. Instead, she was thinking of him in the now, in the present, at this very moment. I'm just glad I didn't respond with what one usually does with such a question, "So, how are you doing?"

Paul had quite the list of serious admonitions in his first epistle to the Thessalonians, chapter 5: "Rejoice always." (v. 16) "Pray without ceasing." (v. 17) Do not quench the Spirit." (v. 19) Tucked in between is verse 18: "in everything give thanks; for this is the will of God in Christ Jesus for you." (1 Thessalonians 5:18, NKJV) That word for "everything" is a Greek word, "panti," which means "all, total, any, whole, every kind of." When people read or hear this verse, they bristle: "How can I be thankful for the death of a child? ". . . for the loss of a spouse?" ". . . for the demise of someone for whom I cared?" Here's the key: Paul never said *"for"* everything, but rather, he said *"in"* everything!

I like to read and hear Dr. Tony Evans. My family and I even attended his church once in Dallas. He has a bit to say about Paul's admonition:

"The Bible says we are to give thanks in everything (1 Thessalonians 5:18). That does not say we have to give thanks for everything. For instance, if your loved one is dying, you don't say, 'Thank You, God, that my loved one is dying.' You say, 'God, I thank You that You are in control of our circumstances, and that you have promised to sustain us with Your love and grace no matter what happens.

"You don't have to give thanks for death because death is part of the curse. It's an enemy, a result of sin."[25]

I may not be appreciative for losing my job or position. I probably won't celebrate a broken bone or serious illness. And I would never express an attitude of gratitude for losing a person in death. But *"in"* that sickness, *"in"* that heartache, *"in"* that loss, I can be thankful to Almighty God—thankful for the heritage, thankful for the life's lessons, thankful for the memories. Bob Hope was not the only one who could sing it. So can we!

CHAPTER NINE

What Will We Do Without Bob?

We'll Keep Going at Our Own Pace

"But as for you, continue in what you have learned and firmly believed, knowing from whom you learned it"

(2 Timothy 3:14, NRSV)

At this writing, our church is going through another transition. Two staff members have retired and another has resigned to accept a position elsewhere. That means I must take a few weeks to get alone and listen for the direction of God. It's almost funny how everyone wants to help you. I get recommendations for the open positions from sincere people who have an uncle who's neighbor two streets over has a cousin whose kid just graduated from a religious institution! Though I appreciate the gesture, there are some things that a pastor can only get from God. The same is true with dealing with death. Well-meaning people want to help, but they are not always helpful.

The one thing I do not want to do with this book is to force anyone to deal with grief a certain way. Bereavement is a very personal thing. We all handle it differently. Just because I was able to move to Nashville and start college two days after I buried my Dad does not mean you can or should do the same. Just because others remarry within a year after they had lost the love of their life does not mean you can do that as well. At the same time, just because it's been ten years and Granny is still in deep grief over the loss of Grandpa doesn't mean you have to do the same.

Here's what I am trying to say: Everyone must journey through the grieving process in their own way and at their own pace. There are no textbook rules that present a timeline of where we should be in our mourning. Everyone is different. No one's emotions are the same as that of another. We have to do only what is right for us and the best place to begin is by deciding where we are on our journey. Robert A. Schuller, son of Dr. Robert H. Schuller of Crystal Cathedral fame, has written a book, *Getting Through What You're Going Through*. In unfolding a personal tragedy of his own, Schuller says "I had to evaluate where I was before I could decide where I was going."[26] With that in mind, allow me to make a few suggestions.

1. Don't let anyone force you to speed-up your grieving.

There are always well-meaning people who want to help someone through the process of grief, yet they have no idea what they are doing. They try to help us get out of our black attire and dark glasses as quickly as possible and back into circulation. Some even try to get a widow or widower back into the dating circuit. Our minds are bombarded with thoughts and questions. *How are they able to just move on when a most wonderful person has left us? How could he have been forgotten so quickly? How could the departed be treated as if she had never existed?* Now, please understand, we don't want to pounce on these people for they are probably, for the most part, innocent—they mean absolutely no harm and have no idea of the hurt they bring.

When my Mom died, there were no "calling hours" at the funeral home. The mortuary was open from 9 a.m. until 9 p.m. and visitation was allowed all day long. I parked it right there for two days at Horis Ward Funeral Home in Decatur, Georgia. The funeral director even came in at closing time and told us he was locking up but we were welcomed to stay as long as we liked. He explained that once we left, we would not be able to re-enter.

I remember how people tried to get me to go home or to get away for awhile. They said I needed to eat or to rest or to do whatever. Though I realized my Mom was gone and that she was with the Lord, I remember thinking, *These are the last two days I will ever see my Mom and I want to stay right by her side.* Healthy or not, right or wrong, good or bad, that's the way I felt. I finally allowed a cousin to talk my sister and me into going out a little while for pizza, but I also remember thinking the whole time we were away, *"I need to get back to the funeral home."* It wasn't as if I would never eat again—I did. It wasn't as if sleep would never come again—it came. I just needed to stay with my Mom and do this at my own pace.

Grieving is an extremely personal experience. What might take six months for one may take six years for another. You and I have to decide when we are ready to do certain things. No one can tell us if and when we should date again. No one can help us decide that it's time to get rid of the clothes or change the room or relocate altogether. We cannot and should not let anyone push us along. There is a process going on that is an important part of the healing. As Jerusha Hull McCormack put it in her book, *Grieving*, "There is no 'right' way to grieve and no 'accepted' schedule for grieving."[27] Please don't let anyone—family, friend, or foe, try to persuade you otherwise.

2. Don't let anyone make you feel badly for your actions.

I'll never forget the night my son was born, April 23, 1987. For over eight years, we had prayed and waited for Tommy. The doctors were not very optimistic that he would ever be possible. As I have already stated, he truly is our miracle. When Tommy came, God came . . . and so did the church choir! They had heard we were at the hospital so they dismissed choir practice and they all showed up. I'm not sure if Cape Fear Memorial Hospital in Wilmington, North Carolina was ever the same.

The next morning, I left my new family for a little while. I went to a nearby restaurant and had a huge breakfast all by myself, my personal way of celebrating, I suppose. Then I knew the mall would be open so I ran by and purchased a gift for my wife and a going-home outfit for my newborn son. I even approached a lady with a baby and kindly informed her that I, too, have one of those (something for which I would probably be arrested today). But I remember one thing that was quite bothersome to me. People were still hurrying to their appointments, traffic was still congested, life was just going on as if nothing had happened. Were they not aware that Thomas Paul Goddard had just made his debut? It was as if I was overcome by this powerful desire to run out into the street and stop traffic to make the birth announcement. Tommy was here and I thought everyone should know.

I also remember that cold, cloudy December day at Georgia Memorial Park when my Mom was laid to rest. Wonderful people shook my hand, some hugged me. One or two slipped a twenty dollar bill into my hand. They whispered kind words and returned to their cars. Continuing to look toward the tent, I watched as gravediggers arrived to do their job. Thinking all were gone, they quickly sprang into action, lowering the casket, sealing the vault, and shoveling the dirt. All the people drove away. Each had offered to do whatever I needed but the majority of them I never saw again. They didn't call. They didn't come by. As a matter of fact, the ones I did see never ever brought up a mere mention of my late Mother. It was as if she had never existed. I learned that after suffering a painful loss in your life, one of the most difficult things to do is to watch as life goes on.

Well meaning people can even say some very hurtful things at a time of loss. Most of it is unintentional, of course, but some statements still sting. Though it's probably a good thing that I don't remember who it was, someone had commented about the engagement and wedding rings on the finger of my mother in the casket. He scolded me that we need to remove them: "You need to take those rings off!" Since Mom never removed her rings and had gone so far as to even making comments about it from time to time, Harold, Vickie, and I had made the decision to leave the rings. We didn't want them. They were hers. Dad agreed. I now realize that people don't always make the best choices during a time of loss and I have questioned that decision a few times over the years, but the three of us had agreed with our Dad's approval. We buried her, rings and all, and felt it was absolutely no one else's business.

I still recall how that man had made me feel. I was hurt. I was angry. I was frustrated. The same feelings come upon those who have been told those typical things that are said after a death. "God knows what's best." "God needed another angel in heaven." "There's a reason for everything." Or one I could hardly believe I heard a preacher recently say at the funeral of a lady in her forties,

"God may have known that she was going to come into terrible sin and so He took her!" To me, that came across as a personal attack on her character, that she would not be able to fight off temptation. I felt badly for the family. Though intended to bring comfort, such statements only wound and leave one feeling comfortless.

To be fair, we have to come to the realization that many have never been where we may be. They haven't walked in our shoes. Many have never suffered a loss of any kind, much less that of someone close. I have been amazed at the number of individuals who have reached their twenties or thirties and have told me they had never lost anyone close, some have never attended a funeral. One, I remember, had never seen a dead body. I guess I just sort of grew up around funeral homes and burial grounds. When my Dad bought six cemetery plots back in the early '60s (at $100 each and had to make payments on them), we spent Sunday afternoons once or twice a month driving that then long trip from Atlanta to Marietta (about 25 miles) to look at our plots! It seemed like it was such a long way. My Grandfather used to make us laugh when he said he didn't want to be buried there because "it was too far to walk back!"

Since many are not around bereavement often, they assume they must "say something" to make the griever feel better and so they end up saying the wrong things, hurtful things. We must try our best to understand this and not allow random comments to drive us into deep depression.

3. Don't let anyone tell you how you should feel.

My father-in-law was a wonderful man. A strong Christian, he and I used to have conversations about the church. He would never tell anyone else his opinion but would share with me what he observed from the fringes. He, too, was a friend of Bob Jung. When Tom's wife, my mother-in-law, was taken to the hospital with a heart attack in the wee hours of the morning, Tom stayed in our guest room. Juanita lived almost a week. After her funeral, Tom was literally unable to go back to their home. At the prompting of Sandie, Tommy, and me, he moved into our house and soon sold his. Our guest room became "Grandpa's room" and he became a stronger part of our immediate family.

My father-in-law had always enjoyed an immaculate lawn and so it was his desire to take responsibility for that of our parsonage. I didn't argue one bit. He mowed, fertilized, did the weed-eating, and he would sit in the driveway on a webbed lawn chair every day, watching his Nelson Rain Train Traveling Sprinkler as it made its crawl down the length of the garden hose. Now that device was made to operate while one was away but Tom felt that he needed to be present, just in case it "jumped track." Some four years after moving in with us, Tom was hospitalized with what we thought was a pulled back muscle. He had pulled the garden hose over his shoulder the previous day and thought that was the reason he was unable to get up. But tests soon indicated multiple myeloma, a cancer that took his life within four months. It had eaten through his vertebra, and that one big tug on the hose had made it snap, the cause of his pain.

His room at the back of our house remained untouched. His clothes continued to hang in the closet. No one really went in there. I knew that when my wife, an only child, was ready, she would go through his things and keep some items and discard others . . . but not until she was ready.

More than a year later, plans were being made for Andrea to come and live with us. A student at Southern Nazarene University, she needed a place to stay for one semester before going to England to study the rest of the year. Only a week before she was to arrive, as if a light had been switched-on, Sandie got excited about fixing-up the guest room. We took Tom's clothes to an Oklahoma City church that has a mission store. We painted the room and bought new bedding. We even moved the furniture around. The room took on a completely new look as well as a different feel. Andrea moved in with great gusto, as only Andrea can, and my wife and I were so very happy.

I knew Sandie would never go through her Dad's things or make any changes until she was ready, and once she was ready, it was for a total change, a whole new look. It was almost as if she suddenly announced one day at Walmart that we were shopping for paint. Until then, no one could make her or anyone else make any changes.

Candy Lightner, founder of Mothers Against Drunk Driving, is mentioned by Phillip Williams as having written, "If there is one thing I have learned . . . it's that we all grieve in our own way and on our own schedule."[28] This chapter can really go two different ways. I have had in mind the one who is grieving, the one who is bereaved. I want that one to know that we all deal with death differently and I want them to never feel guilty or as if something is wrong with them if they are taking longer or even less time to mourn than others do. I guess I'm giving permission to take one's time.

On the other hand, this is a good place to say to those who may be doing the "pushing," to lighten up. Back off and let the one who has suffered a loss get through it in his or her own way. The best thing for a friend or family member to do is just "be there." Offer advice when it is requested. Help wherever you are needed. But instead of insisting on a person to "move on," be patient, understanding, and just be there. Your presence will speak louder than words.

Sandie and I recently had dinner at a little diner in Hagerstown, Indiana. The place had just opened at 4 p.m. and we were the only ones there. After ten minutes or so, three middle-aged ladies came in and sat just a couple of tables over. Since the only sounds in that restaurant were coming from the TV that was showing a rerun of *Bonanza*, we could hear much of their conversation. The waitress approached their table as they were all engaged in laughter. The server made the comment that they were evidently having a good time and one of them replied, "We're celebrating our Mother's birthday." I remember being surprised when I heard that because none of those ladies was old enough to be a mother to the other two. She quickly added, however, "She is no longer with us, but we still celebrate her birthday every year."

I have no idea how long their parent had been gone. I don't know if they had been grieving for months or years. I had never ever seen these women before and I'll probably never ever seen them again. All I know is that three ladies were setting their own pace and had decided to continue to remember their Mom on her special day. You and I must do the same, at our own pace and in our own way.

So Bob Jung is gone, Juanita Waldrep is in heaven, and Paul Goddard will never be back again. We realize we have to deal with those losses as well as many others in our own timing and in our own way. That's easier said than done. How can I accomplish such a monumental task?

I think that question is adequately answered by Dr. Billy Graham: "If there is something else we need more than anything else during grief, it is a friend who stands with us, who doesn't leave us. Jesus is that friend."[29]

CHAPTER TEN

What Will We Do Without Bob?

We'll Keep Touching Others

> . . . that we may be able to comfort those . . . with the comfort
> with which we ourselves are comforted by God.
>
> (2 Corinthians 1:4, NKJV)

As I write the words of this chapter, I am sitting in a sixth floor hotel room in Denver. It's cold outside. The snow on the ground matches the snow-capped mountains which I can see on the horizon. I called someone back home today on my cell phone to check on a new mother and her newborn baby. I had been there at the hospital only hours before I flew out of town. The baby was born while I was there but not without some frightening moments. Both Mom and little girl are now fine, thank the good Lord. I also talked with another friend today, one whose grown and married son is struggling through some extremely tough treatments of chemotherapy. Sometimes it seems the cure is worse than the cancer. Although I'm away with my family for a quick weekend vacation, I guess there's something built within that says we should keep checking on and touching the lives of others.

I think that is especially true for those who have suffered the death of a loved one. When we hear that someone has been suddenly left behind, our heart immediately goes out to them. We pray for them. We send flowers to the funeral home or the residence. Depending on how close the relationship, we might even call or pay a personal visit to the survivor. These are all acts of expressing sympathy. Perhaps we've never been through that. Maybe we don't really know how he or she feels. All we can do is imagine the pain, the loneliness, the awful feeling of loss. We are *sympathizing* with that person.

But maybe it's not like that at all. Perhaps we *do* know how they feel. It may be that we also have lost someone close to us and we understand firsthand what they are experiencing. We know the sting. We have felt the heartache. We certainly understand the stages of grief that our friend is experiencing. This is more than *sympathy*—it's *empathy*. We *empathize* when we know exactly how a person feels because we ourselves have been there.

Those of us who can empathize need to reach out and touch the lives of those who are experiencing bereavement. This is not just a nice thing to do—it's biblical: "Blessed be the God and Father of our Lord Jesus Christ, the Father of mercies and God of all comfort, who comforts us in all our tribulation, that we may be able to comfort those who are in any trouble, with the comfort with which we ourselves are comforted by God." (2 Corinthians 1:3-4) Since God's Holy Spirit, the Comforter, has helped us, we can and should help someone else. So what can we do to help others through their grief?

1. We can be there.

By far the most important lesson I have learned as a pastor at the time of death is to just be present. This holds true for the sick room, the funeral home, even the times after the interment is history. In those situations most people think they have to say something, that they should offer some profound words of wisdom that will dull the pain. I never learned those words as a ministerial student in college, nor seminary, and as a young pastor I came to realize that there are no magic words.

Funeral directors find they can call on me when they have pastorless families and I often officiate memorial services for people I never knew. Then there have naturally been a list of church members I did know and I stood over their open graves and tried to say a few words to comfort those left behind. I've buried saints of God who almost lived a century and I've helped young parents say goodbye to those so tiny that didn't ever have a chance at life. Through all of my experiences over thirty years of pastoring, I still know of no words that are adequate. The greatest lesson I've learned is to just "be there."

One of my associate pastors and I recently called on a couple in their home. The night before, their son was on a moped and I'm still not sure if he ran a stop sign or what happened, but he pulled out into the path of a speeding police car that was responding to a call. Killed at the age of twenty-two! What could Rex and I say that could possibly make this couple feel better? I didn't know then, nor do I now. All we could do is be there, offer a prayer, and let them know they were not alone.

We often articulate the wrong things or we just stay away, all because we don't know the "magic words." Don't try to conjure up something to say because most of the time there really is nothing that can be said. Don't try to search for places to go or things to do that will help one get their mind off the pressing reality because such cannot be accomplished. Just be there. Say nothing. Your presence will speak for you.

We watched Cortney grow up in our youth group, become a college student, then a children's pastor. She is also a wonderful wife and mother. While I was working on this very chapter, Cortney called me on my cell phone. She now serves another church on another district and so our visits are really few and far between. She was headed to the hospital because the family of someone had been called in, the lady was dying. Cortney's pastor was tied up at a different hospital and so she called me to get some guidance as she drove to the death room. My best advice to her was to just "be there." I told her to speak very little but to make her presence known. That's the best any of us can do.

I did that just last night. News reached me that a young mother only a few doors from our church was accidentally shot and flown by helicopter to Indianapolis, where she underwent surgery for most of the night and morning. She does not attend our church, nor does she attend any church, but she's a part of our community and our church is in that neighborhood to minister. I drove to Methodist Hospital in Indianapolis and found her room in the trauma ward. I walked in, introduced myself, and told the lady and her husband that our church would be praying for her. Then I left. I only stayed three or four minutes. I didn't even pray because I did not feel led to do so. I was just there and they seemed to appreciate it.

Job was one who experienced tremendous pain and suffering. He lost all that he had—his home, his family, his servants, even his health. We've all heard of "Job's friends," and how they were not so comforting. At first, however, they seemed to do alright. The scriptures says, "So they sat down with him on the ground seven days and seven nights, and no one spoke a word to him, for they saw that his grief was very great." (Job 2:13) So far, so good.

They just sat there for a whole week and kept their mouths shut. Then they unfortunately started to speak, going so far as to place blame on Job for his tragic circumstances. Gregory Clapper comments: "These friends would have done better if they had never opened their mouths and simply wept with Job."[30]

So lesson number one is definitely to practice one's presence. Though he is referring to pastors during the time of someone's loss, the words of Harold Ivan Smith apply to anyone: "The best gift you offer is your presence. Your presence says, 'You do not have to go through this loss alone.'"[31]

2. We can listen.

A person experiencing the pain of loss has definitely something to say. As a matter of fact, they have something they *need* to say. The want to talk about their loved one. Their desire is to reminisce, to remember days gone by. It appears to be helpful for them to recall the last thing they did together, the last words he spoke, the last time she did whatever. The griever simply needs someone to listen.

How many times have I sat in a person's home or in a funeral home and have listened to "their story?" I have heard them repeat it again and again, each time someone new would arrive to visit and offer comfort. I've noticed how most people allow the bereaved one to speak but I've also taken note of those who seem to be uncomfortable with the sad account. Those are the ones who try to silence the one who is hurting. I don't think it's as much for the pain of the survivor as it is for the listener who doesn't want to hear.

My phone rang late one night. The elderly lady was calling from the emergency room where her husband had just passed away. I got dressed and drove the thirty minutes to the hospital in

Winchester, Indiana. As I drove, I recalled the last few times I had called on him in their home. I remembered a recent visit. We sat together at the kitchen table, I in my coat and tie, he in his Oshkosh overalls, and he said, "Preacher, one of these days they'll bring me to the church in a pine box and I want you to say some words over me." That was his way of asking me to preach his funeral.

When I arrived at the hospital, they escorted me to the room where the body was. The widow was still sitting close by. She was alone. She stood as I entered the room and we hugged and we cried. We sat down and I held her hand as she began to tell me what had happened, the events of the evening that had led to the 911 call.

Soon the funeral director arrived. Since they all lived in a small community, the longtime undertaker was very acquainted with this family. He hugged the widow and then he asked her, "He had a rough time, didn't he?" She then started in on her story, her detailed explanation of what had transpired, when the mortician suddenly cut her off: "Okay, I have work to do. I'll call you in the morning." With that, he quickly started removing the body from the bed to place onto the gurney. Within minutes, he was gone. Though it didn't seem to bother this sweet lady, I was appalled at the rudeness of the small town undertaker. This dear lady had something to say and the least we can do is listen.

It is imperative that we become good listeners. We owe it to that one who is in pain. We don't have to ask lots of questions. We don't even have to understand. We should merely let them talk. Hold their hand while they share with you and refrain from telling your own similar story. Let them know how much you really do care about them and what they are experiencing.

3. We can be part of their grief.

Grief is not just the pain and suffering. It's not just the experience of loss.

Grief includes those who come alongside to help. That would be you and me. We can be part of the grieving process for someone who is hurting. Especially helpful are those of us who have been there, those of us who understand. We can be used of God to minister to people in pain. And yes, you are needed. Grief counselors Deborah E. Bowen and Susan L. Strickler acknowledge the help of others during loss of their own: "We needed the help of many others to make our way through the morass of pain."[32]

Have you been there? Perhaps you are there right now. It's very important that we take what we learn and in turn help someone else as they cringe through the chaos. Many times I will introduce someone who is in bereavement to a person in the church who had also lost a spouse or someone who also buried a child. The ministry of comforting is really a two-way street. As we help someone else in need, someone who is now where we once were, we are also recipients of ministry. Aren't you grateful for the presence of the Holy Spirit, the Comforter, who helps us through those terrible times?

Conclusion

"Finally, my brethren, rejoice in the Lord."
(Philippians 3:1, NKJV)

Roy Disney said of his brother, Walt, "The death of Walt Disney is a loss to all the people of the world."[33] Although that's a tremendously bold statement, I suppose you could declare it fairly true. From the several mentions in this book, one can obviously tell that I'm a Disney fan and the theme parks are two of my favorite places in the world. Disneyland opened on July 15, 1955 on a site of 160 acres near Anaheim, California and over the years has welcomed over 600 million guests. Then on October 1, 1971 Walt Disney World opened near Orlando, Florida, occupying over 30,000 acres and has been named the world's largest and most-visited recreational resort. That's quite the legacy that was left behind.

But we all had a Walt or a Brenda or a Reba or a Bob. He or she may not have a theme park named for them, nor a shrine of any kind built to their name. But they were ours and now they're gone and we are affected.

The writer to the Hebrews spoke of a "cloud of witnesses," a grandstand that's filled with the saints who have gone before us. They are rooting for us. They are cheering us on. They are saying that they made it all the way to the finish line and so can we. "Therefore, since we are surrounded by so great a cloud of witnesses, let us also lay aside every weight and the sin that clings so closely, and let us run with perseverance the race that is set before us, looking to Jesus . . ." (Hebrews 12:1-2, NRSV)

Some of us may have more on the other side than we do on this side. We already have an investment in heaven. This is no time to give up. This is not a day to quit. We must square our shoulders, hold our heads up, and continue to live life to the fullest. How can we do that when we are grieving the loss of someone we loved? Verse 2 of Hebrews 11 answers that question: "looking unto Jesus." We cannot do it on our own but the Lord Jesus wants to help us so that we won't be "troubled." (John 14:1)

The Apostle Paul wrote the good people of Corinth, "Praise be to the God and Father of our Lord Jesus Christ, the Father of compassion and the God of all comfort, who comforts us in all our troubles, so that we can comfort those in any trouble with the comfort we ourselves have received from God." (2 Corinthians 1:3-4, NIV) We receive comfort from the Comforter Himself so that we, in turn, can comfort others suffering a loss themselves. We can actually turn our mourning into ministry.

What will we do without Bob? We'll just keep on keeping on. There will be times of tears. We'll experience some difficult days. We may do fine for weeks only to have the reality of our loss hit us all over again like it's brand new. There will be many moments when we just don't think we can make it. But the good news is that with the power of the Holy Spirit, we can keep Bob alive in our minds and hearts forever until we meet again.

Notes

Chapter 1
1. Harold Ivan Smith, *When Your People Are Grieving* (Kansas City, MO: Beacon Hill Press, 2001), 12.
2. Elizabeth Harper Neeld, *Seven Choices: Finding Daylight After Loss Shatters Your World* (New York: Warner Books, 2003), 26.
3. Steve Griffiths, *God of the Valley* (Minneapolis, MN: Augsburgh Books, 2003), ix.

Chapter 2
4. Harold Ivan Smith, *A Decembered Grief* (Kansas City, MO: Beacon Hill Press, 1999), 50.
5. Warren Wiersbe, *Be Joyful* (Wheaton, IL: Victor Books, 1974), 14.
6. Francois-Marie Arouet Voltaire, http//www.ThinkExist.com (accessed 2010).
7. E.E. Cummins, *The Quote Garden,* http//www.quotegarden.com (accessed 2010).

Chapter 3
8. William Barclay, *And He Had Compassion* (Valley Forge, PA: Judson Press, 1976), 200.
9. Gregory S. Clapper, *When the World Breaks Your Heart,* (Nashville, TN: Upper Room Books, 1999), 104-105.
10. Rick Warren, *The Purpose Driven Life* (Grand Rapids, MI: Zondervan, 2002) 53.

Chapter 4
11. Gregory S. Clapper, *When the World Breaks Your Heart*, 17.
12. Ibid, 23.
13. H.B. London (Southwest Oklahoma District Nazarene Pastors-Spouses Retreat, Oklahoma City, OK), September 28, 2007.
14. Liz Cowan Furman, *How To Plan a Funeral* (Kansas City, MO: Beacon Hill Press, 2008), 13.

Chapter 5
15. Rick Weinberg, *Derek and dad finish Olympic 400 together, ESPN Counts Down the 100 Most Memorable Moments of the Past 25 Years*, http://sports.espn.go.com/vespn25/story?page=moments/94 (accessed July 16, 2011).
16. W. Phillip Keller, *A Shepherd Looks at Psalm 23* (Grand Rapids, MI: 2007), 103.

Chapter 6
17. Leo Rosten, ed. *Leo Rosten's Treasury of Jewish Quotations* (New York: Bantam, 1980), 449
18. Gregory S. Clapper, *When the World Breaks Your Heart*, 32.
19. Harold Ivan Smith, *A Decembered Grief*, 16.
20. Gregory S. Clapper, *When the World Breaks Your Heart*, 40.

Chapter 7
21. *The Oklahoman*, (Oklahoma City, OK), November 22, 2007
22. Helen Fitzgerald, *The Mourning Handbook* (New York: Simon and Shuster, 1994), 107.

Chapter 8
23. Stan Toler, *Total Quality Life* (Indianapolis, IN: The Wesleyan Publishing House: 2007), 82.
24. Ibid, 82-83.
25. Tony Evans, *The Battle is the Lord's* (Chicago: Moody Press, 1998), 391-392.

Chapter 9
26. Robert A. Schuller, *Getting Through What You're Going Through* (Nashville, TN: Thomas Nelson, 1986), 1.
27. Jerusha Hull McCormack, *Grieving* (Brewster, MA: 2006), 129.
28. Phillip W. Williams, *When a Loved One Dies: Meditations For the Journey Through Grief (Minneapolis, MN: Augsburg Press, 1995),* 288.
29. Billy Graham, *Hope For the Troubled Heart* (Dallas: Word, 1991), 116.

Chapter 10
30. Gregory S. Clapper, *When the World Breaks Your Heart*, 38.
31. Harold Ivan Smith, *When Your People Are Grieving,* 33
32. Deborah E. Bowen and Susan L. Strickler, *A Good Friend for Bad*

Conclusion
33. Neal Gabler, *Walt Disney* (New York: Vintage Books, 2006), 631.

Author Bio

Danny Goddard was born and raised in Atlanta, GA. He received his B.A. degree from Trevecca Nazarene College in Nashville, TN, a Masters of Church Management from Olivet Nazarene University in Kankakee, IL, and a Masters of Divinity from Nazarene Theological Seminary in Kansas City, MO. Danny is also a graduate of the Nazarene School of Large Church Management.

An ordained elder in the Church of the Nazarene, Danny has pastored Churches of the Nazarene in Indiana, Nebraska, North Carolina, and Oklahoma. He is presently senior pastor at First Church of the Nazarene in New Castle, Indiana.

Danny and his wife, Sandie, have one son, Tommy, who resides with his wife, Micha, in Oklahoma City. Danny is the author of *Pastoral Care in Times of Death and Dying* (Beacon Hill Press, 2009) A fulltime pastor for over three decades, Danny feels a special calling to minister in times of death.

www.ingramcontent.com/pod-product-compliance
Lightning Source LLC
LaVergne TN
LVHW021400080426
835508LV00020B/2368